Palermo: Travels in the City of Happiness

Art, Architecture & History
in Sicily's Ancient Captial

2015

Palermo: Travels in the City of Happiness
Art, Architecture & History in Sicily's Ancient Capital
by Allan Langdale

Cover design by Allan Langdale

Cover photo: The mosaic of Ceres from the Panificio of Salvatore Morello, Palermo, 1908.

Book formatting and cover layout by Agatha Malina (studio-upstairs.com)

First Edition, 2015

Published in the United States of America

ISBN# 978-0-578-16934-7

TABLE OF CONTENTS

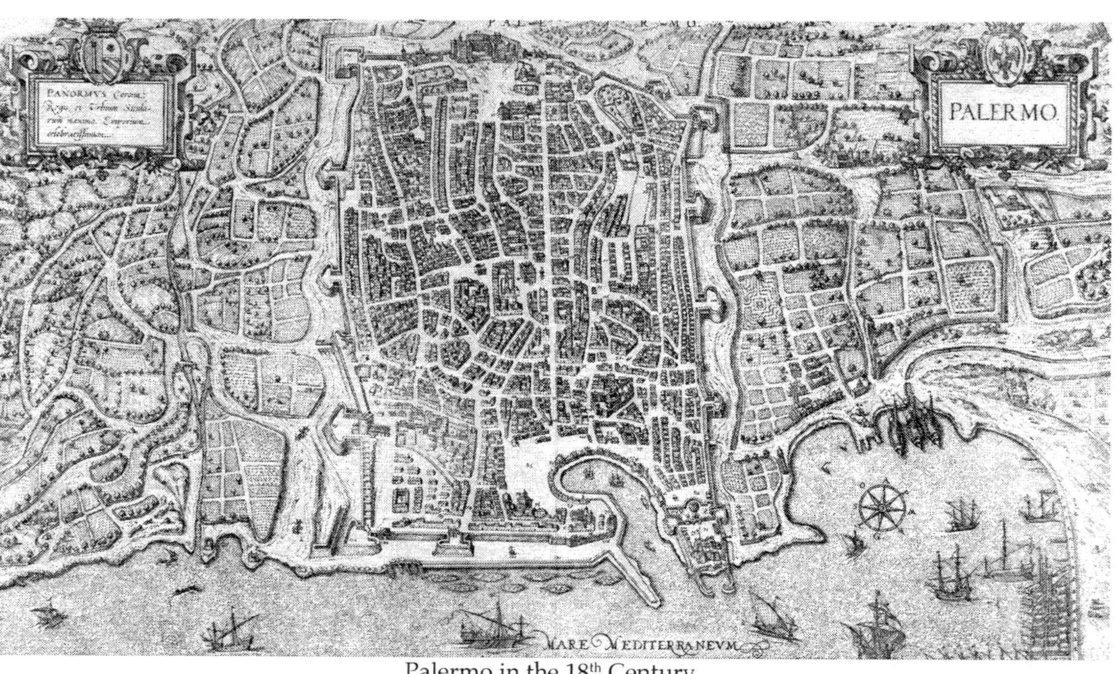

Palermo in the 18th Century

FOREWORD

As with all projects that take years to complete there are innumerable people to thank. Cassandra and Philip Grant, Suzanne Duca and Ross Quigley, Peter Sturman and Hui Shu Lee, Jim and Hawley Kusch, Patrice Bailey, and Bill Heid and June Gordon have all offered much appreciated hospitality. Writers need other writers' encouragement and here I've also had sympathetic friends, among them Roger Crowley, Elizabeth McKenzie, Constance Penley, Michael Covino, and Robert Raisch. Giulia Centineo was a great help early on, sharing her enthusiasm and memories of the city she grew up in and helpful, too, in introducing me to her friends who still live in Palermo: Umberto Santino, Michele Anselmi, and Claudia Oliva, all of whom generously offered their time while I was doing research in their magnificent city.

Many others have supported me in various ways. Chris Husted has remained an ever positive friend, Jena Lewis and A. J. de Dios have always been generous, and Shelley Stamp cheerfully backed me through my many obligatory professional realignments. Friends in Palermo who gave me support include the gang at Casa di Amici: Claudia, Santo, Alexandra, Clement, John, and Antonio.

Agatha Malina was invaluable when it came to laying out the covers and manuscript.

I wouldn't have been able to research this book without the people who work at the Interlibrary Loan department of McHenry Library at UC Santa Cruz. Thanks to them all for chasing down the obscurest of volumes.

I've never met Bill Bryson, but his travel books encouraged me to think it was possible to write a book that was entertaining even though you also learned a lot from it. I'd also like to thank Zegrahm Expeditions and Smithsonian Journeys for giving me opportunities to travel.

My greatest appreciation goes to my mother, Nancy, whose unflagging support does much to sustain me, to say nothing of her ace editing skills.

☙

INTRODUCTION

I first visited Palermo in 1981 as a twenty-two-year-old backpacker. I'd sewn a Canadian flag on my rucksack, not because I was a wary American but because I was actually Canadian. I remember trudging through the squalor of Palermo's old quarter and not seeing a single tourist, which intrigued me because, even though the city's historical center was in a state of picturesque decay, the buildings were nevertheless magnificent. I recall wandering aimlessly, but in a state of continuous wonder. I had the Palatine Chapel, Palermo's biggest attraction, all to myself. That first visit was short, only a couple of days, as I had to get to Trapani to catch the once-weekly ferry to Tunis. But that short visit stuck with me for years, the images of the city strangely indelible. Palermo's dire situation—something I was only vaguely aware of at the time—didn't change much through the 1980s and 90s, when the city suffered mafia warfare and violent reactions to anti-mafia campaigns. Fear kept visitors away.

In 1991 Fernanda Eberstadt wrote on Palermo for *The New Yorker.* Her article was infused with despair; she saw a crumbling city, a "wild, unvisited place", yet at the same time observed that it was "also one of the most ravishing cities in the world, planted by a geographer with an eye for high drama." Alexander Stille's *Excellent Cadavers* came out in 1995, focusing on the anti-mafia prosecutors Giovanni Falcone and Paolo Borsellino. Peter Robb's *Midnight in Sicily* came out soon after and I revisited Palermo through its pages, but was saddened by the terrors the book gives such a captivating account of. These bestsellers defined many peoples' attitude towards the city, but they didn't describe my Palermo, which was a city blessed with wondrous art and architecture. Whenever I encouraged people to visit they would always raise their eyebrows and ask me about the mafia. It was as if I'd suggested they take a vacation to the Gaza strip. Yet today you're far less likely to be a victim of crime in Palermo than in many American cities. As for crossing the street, well, it is Italy after all.

My Palermo was an ancient city that for over three thousand years had been a vibrant cultural center. For most of its history it's been one of the great cities of the Mediterranean, and even with the recent uptick in tourism, Palermo is still one of Italy's most authentic cities, as yet unspoiled by too many visitors. When Eberstadt wrote her *New Yorker* piece, someone said, "You are writing a story about Palermo? Then it will be a tragedy." But Palermo has successfully reinvented itself in the past twenty years. Earlier neglect is being superseded by care and attention, with several conservation campaigns recently completed and others under way as citizens realize the value of the city's cultural history, among them Mayor Leoluca Orlando, who did much to turn the tide, instigating the *Primavera di Palermo,* "the Palermo Spring." The city is reclaiming a sobriquet it enjoyed centuries ago, *La Felice,* 'The Happy'. The glories of the medieval Norman period, the Baroque masterpieces, the splendid works of Art Nouveau, and even Fascist-era art and architecture are accompanied by a vibrant multicultural environment, all enlivened by the city's religious festivals.

This more enthusiastic evaluation of Palermo I share with many travelers through history. One of the most pleasurable aspects of my work was discovering the accounts of visitors from the past and placing their experiences alongside my own. Through these voices a richer portrait of the city emerges, one which gives a greater sense of Palermo's enduring grandeur.

The following chapters are an account of a week spent in Palermo in the spring of 2014, augmented with snippets from earlier visits. I've tried to organize these daily chapters into what could be actual itineraries, though in practice they'd be easier to read about than do. I've tried to map out my experiences of the city—its spaces, its people, its history, its works of art—into a series of urban expeditions. Half way through writing, I also realized that this book was also my treatise on travel. I like cities as subjects because I like to become immersed in a place, not simply to check off the sights, so that there's at least one café where I can walk in and they already know what I want.

This book is for tourists, for fellow travelers, but it's also offered in friendship to the citizens of Palermo who love their history and who have met the challenge of preserving their wonderful city's heritage for the rest of us.

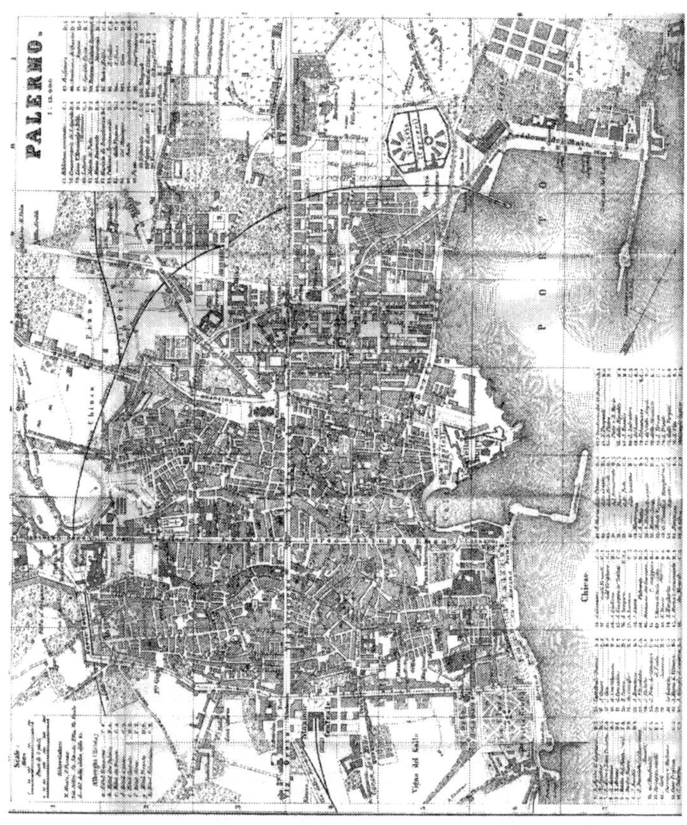

Palermo in the 19th Century

ARRIVAL

> *...Palermo, the ancient seate of the Sicilian kings: stiled the Happie, for the delightful situation; now adorned with goodly buildings, and frequented by students.*

-George Sandys, *A Relation of a Journey,* 1610

> *No words can express the hazy brilliancy which hung around the coasts, as on a most beautiful noon we neared Palermo. He who has once seen it will never forget it.*

-Goethe, *Italian Travels,* 1787

By the time I got to Palermo I'd lost track of how long I'd gone without sleep, wedged into economy class from Santa Barbara to Los Angeles, Los Angeles to Frankfurt, Frankfurt to Rome and, finally, Rome to Sicily. Then, due to traffic, it took another hour to get to the hotel. I checked in at the Excelsior, which in Latin means 'ever upwards', apparently referring to my credit card bill. It gave me a sense of security I was at the time quite willing to pay for. Years ago, in my early twenties, I'd slept on a park bench in Palermo's Villa Giulia gardens, my backpack tied to a light post with a sock. I'd awoken in the night and seen the world's largest rat, the size of a small terrier, ambling along the path. Whatever nostalgia I had for my youthful travels, and I had plenty, the backpacker's rustic accommodation wasn't part of it. I was relieved to have clean sheets, a full bathroom, and a room free of gigantic rodents.

I deposited my luggage and set out for a stroll. I couldn't sleep anyway, fatigued though I was. I went to the English Gardens beside the hotel and sat below the bronze equestrian statue of Garibaldi who, from a certain angle, looked like a tour guide on horseback exclaiming, "Look at that palm tree!" He was ignored by a group of teenagers even though in 1860 he was the Liberator of Sicily with his red-shirted Expedition of the Thousand. His arm is raised in an imperial gesture to ideals that have little relevance for sexting and tweeting kids. Why should they ponder this valiant figure and the battle for the city that he led over a hundred and fifty years ago, or care that, in the same year, at the age of fifty three, he married an eighteen-year-old girl, Guiseppina Raimondi, who, after the solemn nuptials, informed him she was pregnant with another man's child? No wonder he wanted to go out and conquer something. At the foot of the statue a bronze lion—metaphor for Garibaldi—chomps on a heavy chain, breaking the bonds of Bourbon tyranny; the French monarchal kind, not the Kentucky, liquid kind. The bench beneath Garibaldi's verdigris effigy was a pleasant spot to make a quick reconnoiter of my map. It was 6:00 pm and I needed to stay awake until 9:00, when I'd allow myself a hot bath before collapsing in sheets with a thread count that would make Nero blush, hopefully waking tomorrow with my physiological clock reset.

It took me a block or two to get my land legs back, but I was soon striding cheerfully up the Via della Libertà and feeling it rightly named indeed. The street is adorned with grand buildings from the nineteenth century. There used to be more of them, but in the 1960s several were demolished, lining the pockets of corrupt politicians and mafiosi who benefitted from lucrative government subsidies for new construction. Many of Palermo's noble edifices were replaced with generic concrete high rises. Several of the old palaces had been damaged in the Allied bombing in 1943 and that, too, was a contributing factor in the decline of the city's architecture. There are still signs of the war damage today. Despite the down-on-its-luck bits, however, this noble city, almost three-thousand years old and having witnessed a procession of occupiers—Greeks, Phoenicians, Romans, Byzantines, Arabs, Normans, French, Spanish, and, some Sicilians might say, Italians—shows real signs of vitality. Palermo has had many names through history: *Ziz* ('The Flower') to the Phoenicians—who founded the city in the 8th century BCE—*Panormus* ('Port for All') to the ancient Greeks; *Balarm* or *Balarmuh* to the Arabs, who also referred to it as *Madinat Siqilliyya* ('The City of Sicily'), or, simply, *al-Madina*, ('The City'); and the nickname

La Felice ('The Happy'). In the Middle Ages Palermo was referred to as 'The City of the Threefold Speech', since public notices were posted in Greek, Arabic, and Latin; meanwhile, the Normans used French as their court language. Sometimes Hebrew was added to documents, as many Jews also resided in the city. Through all these ages Palermo has been a fascinating place. Little wonder, given its strategic position in the middle of the Mediterranean.

The midday siesta, the *pisolino,* was over and shops were opening for the second time in the day. The streets were loud and lively. Palermitan teens zipped about in candy-colored scooters, jousting with pedestrians and obliging even black-clad widows with walking sticks to step lively. Breezes from the Tyrrhenian Sea had ventilated the piazzas for the evening *passeggiata,* when young and old congregate in the city's squares and walk along the main thoroughfare, closed to cars every evening for the purpose. The tree-lined Via della Libertà, which continues south as the Via Ruggiero Settimo, extends further still into the Via Maqueda, making a wonderful two-kilometer long pedestrian zone. I walked slowly, happily, with nowhere in particular to go. Shop windows glowed optimistically, exhibiting a rainbow of chic wares. Grocery stores offered bargains in splashy reds; a Nigerian man sold sunglasses off a sheet on the sidewalk, creating an impromptu storefront for knock-off Ray Bans at five Euros apiece (bargained down from fifty!); a pharmacy proclaimed its sanitary ambience with bright lights and its medicinal vocation with green crosses. Persuaded, I entered and bought some toothpaste from a young man in a brilliant white lab coat with the name 'Enrico' stitched in red cursive over his heart. Was he aware that in 1241 Frederick II of Sicily was the first ruler to legally segregate the practices of apothecary and physician? Enrico was so good looking, a veritable Palermitan Valentino, I imagined the women of the city traversing the town to see him. Doors would swing open, squeaking: "Enrico!" followed by a revealing lean over the counter and whispers punctuated by the sensuous cooing that in all of nature only flirting Italian women can produce. Enrico blushes, trying to maintain a starched professionalism. I imagine some men did the same. To which summons Enrico responded I know not. Toothpaste was all I required at the moment.

Having quickly and cheaply satisfied that particularly North American urge to purchase something to formalize one's arrival in a foreign country, with a newfound sense of belonging I clutched the pharmacy bag—touched by Enrico!—and stepped up my pace, though never wandering far from the reassuring axis of the Via Libertà, along which lay a direct path back to the commodious sanctuary of the Excelsior. I indulged in the traveler's forgivable voyeurism as lights came on in flats, observing people going about their daily business: watching television; doing dishes; and from their balconies gathering up colorful banners of laundry dried crisp by midday's desiccating zephyrs. Whilst witnessing such cozy scenes of daily life I found myself winding down quickly, and as the streetlamps began to glow and the *passeggiata* of the Palermitani began I dragged myself back to the hotel, sad to miss the spectacle but much anticipating that expansive, and expensive, bed.

ଓ

DAY ONE

*It [Palermo] is the metropolis of these islands,
combining the benefits of wealth and splendor,
and having all you could wish for of beauty...
It is an ancient and elegant city, magnificent
and gracious and seductive to look upon... the
King, to whom it is his world, has embellished
it to perfection...may Allah destroy it.*

-Ibn Jubayr, *Travels*, 1185

*Palermo's claim to attention lies more in what
has been than what it is, or rather in the intimate
complication of the two. [This is true] not only
in the great historical buildings, in castle, church
and palace, but in squalid streets and dingy yards,
in narrow alleys and malodorous courts, [the
traveler] will light on noble or pathetic relics—
doorway and window, gate, arch and column—that
make old ages live again. And these old ages are
so various, so crowded with interest and import,
the races, creeds, ideals, systems of which Sicily
has been the meeting place and the battleground,
which she has attracted, amalgamated, assimilated,
are so diverse, the past and present are so subtly
interwoven by a thousand threads of continuity
and consequence, that the life of today is hardly
separable from the complex tapestry behind it.*

-Spencer Musson, *Sicily*, 1911

Great cities have distinctive atmospheres, most accessible in the morning when there's a dewy silence over all, Palermo no less than any other. Wide boulevards soon to be congealed with unruly traffic are preternaturally tranquil before sunrise. To walk the pre-dawn streets of cities like London or Athens is to witness great giants easing out of slumber as their avenues gradually fill. It was in those very waking hours that I found myself walking up the Via della Libertà on a splendid clear morning with the rising sun casting a soft glow on Palermo's streets, eerily quiet, like one of Atget's famous photographs of the vacant streets of Paris. I'd awoken at 5:00 am, strangely energized, thrown some things in a backpack and with boyish glee slipped past the dozing concierge like a truant from a boarding school.

The occasional taxi whizzed by me, ferrying someone to an early-bird flight to Rome. A truck grumbled, breaking the silence and ducking into a slippery alley to unload its burden of crates. There was a warm, comforting smell from a bakery; I peeked in and trays of pastries were being drawn from glowing ovens. Salty mists had stolen into the city, but soon a crisp breeze from the mountains cascaded gently over the long slope above the city called the Conca d'Oro or 'The Shell of Gold', and bore the opulent scent of orange blossom.

One of the greatest literary evocations of the sense of smell in all of literature has a Palermo connection; an early passage in Giuseppe di Lampedusa's 1958 novel *The Leopard* (*Il Gattopardo*) where the author describes the conflicting scents in the Prince of Salina's garden, as if they embody both the hope and despair, the beauty and viciousness of Sicily at that moment in its history when Garibaldi came with his Thousand to overturn the Sicilian feudal social order. The passage, pages long, opens with the cloying scent of flowers and ends with the stench of a soldier's decaying corpse. When the journalist Fernanda Eberstatd came to Palermo in 1990 she also found the smells of the city memorable: "Rich smells, for Palermo is a city more pungent than any Chinatown—a city in whose manifold smells you can rediscover a buried, pre-hygienic Europe: the reek of animal guts, rotting fish, oranges, shit, ammonia, cats; the burned splendor of *torrefazione* (roasting coffee beans); the smell of baking bread, wood smoke, roasting chestnuts (this is an autumn-winter smell; in spring it's orange blossoms), anise, sweat, garlic, seaweed, tobacco, gasoline, incense." My olfactory recollections from the early 1980s concurred with her description, but in the intervening years the more egregious of these odors have been eradicated while happily leaving many of the nicer ones intact. There's probably a whole list of European Union rules against stinkiness that Palermo had in the interim been obliged to address.

There's a haunting anecdote, also involving the sense of smell, told by the French writer Guy de

Maupassant, who visited Palermo in the spring of 1885. He was lodged at the famous Hotel des Palmes and found out that the German composer Richard Wagner had stayed there a few years before, writing his opera *Parsifal*. De Maupassant asks the concierge if he can see Wagner's suite, hoping that some remnant spirit of the artist's greatness will inspire him. At first he feels nothing of Wagner's ghost, but upon opening the wardrobe he is struck by the unmistakable fragrance of rosewater. The concierge explains that Wagner ordered his silk sheets—Wagner fetishized that particular textile—imbued with the scent daily, and had hung them in that closet. De Maupassant writes that he "inhaled that breath of flowers, enclosed in that piece of furniture, forgotten there, a captive," thus literally finding the inspiration he yearned for. De Maupassant didn't know it, but another great artist had been in that same room. Auguste Renoir had done a sketch of the composer for a portrait which now hangs in the Musée d'Orsay in Paris.

I was headed this morning to the old port, called *La Cala,* to get a view of Palermo's famous Monte Pellegrino. Many nineteenth-century painters and photographers had recorded this geographic icon and I wanted to see the legendary vista for myself. I espied an orange bus with *101-Stazione,* the direction of the train station, on the route panel. It was just the bus I needed, so I hopped aboard. There were only four people on it. A prim, studious woman in her seventies, trim and alert, sat reading a paperback book. She was dressed in clothes that would've been stylish in the 1960s. Her bookmark, decorated with a blue tassel, had the Virgin Mary on it. Maybe she was going to work. Perhaps she volunteered. All her life, I imagined, she'd been the first person in the office, or perhaps a library or archive; on Sundays the first to church so she could visit the saints' icons without distraction, her devotions unwavering over the decades.

A slim young man with a wan complexion, red eyes and spiked hair, seemed to be recovering from a dosage of something the old lady would no doubt have disapproved of. He had chrome studs in his nose and a series of steel loops along the helix of his left ear, one of which was inflamed. A tattoo of indeterminate design peeked out from the upturned collar of his black leather jacket, it, too, copiously riveted. He tugged on his delinquent earring and scowled.

A pleasant woman, about thirty, balanced on her knee a wriggly little boy, scrubbed and sweet, as the bus lurched through an intersection. She licked her fingers and tried to paste down a wayward sprig of his hair, which, like the rest of him, refused to submit. Her brow furrowed. No wedding ring. She had the Look-of-Continuous-Worry of the single mother; a delicate gold cross hung stoically around her neck. St Margaret of Cortona, who lived in the thirteenth century, is the patron saint of single mothers. Although I am not religious, I directed a prayer to her, and as I looked up again she smiled weakly, as if she'd intercepted the transmission and appreciated the thought. The little boy released a spontaneous peal of warbling laughter, as if he, in his childish innocence, had sensed that St Margaret had just changed the used gum wrapper in his mother's purse into a winning lottery ticket, and we all smiled, even the septuagenarian, early-rising archivist, whose youthful beauty was suddenly revealed again in her bright, charitable eyes.

You can never claim to know a city without using all its forms of public transport. One of my favorite cities is Istanbul because it has old trains, busses, electric tramways (even one railway that goes up a steep tunnel on cogs), streetcars on Istiklal Street and, best of all, the ferries that traverse the Bosporus, dodging the hair-raising cross-traffic of immense tankers and cruise ships going to or coming from the Black Sea—an intercontinental boat ride for less than a $1.50. Now there's a subway that goes under that famed waterway. You can see the real people of the city doing something they do every day, going to work, and you can be doubly happy that, for once, you don't have to.

I got off the bus at the Quattro Canti ('Four Corners') and made a beeline to the seaside, passing through the Palermo Gate, also known as the Porta Felice or Gate of Happiness. It has no top, just two flanking piers, purportedly so the towering cart of the reliquary of Santa Rosalia, Palermo's patron saint, can pass through it during her festival. I walked out to a seaside park called the Villa a Mare and had a wonderful, unimpeded view of Monte Pellegrino gently lit by the warming sun. Spencer Musson, who visited Palermo in 1909, penned a description I won't attempt to compete with, poetically evoking the effects of light and weather upon the city's most distinctive landform: "[Monte Pellegrino's] bare, weather–worn surface is peculiarly susceptible of atmospheric effect; dawn, with gentle, hesitating touch, lays delicate tints upon it, noon robes it in golden haze, the purple shadows of the clouds loiter idly in its hollows; fleecy mists from the sea drape it in ghostly white, dank winds wrap it in a clinging shroud, storms cast their black mantle upon it; the sinking sun fires it with fugitive and flaming passion, then leaves it in a shadowy phantom, looming grey and vague, or glimmering pale and spectral in the cold magic of moon and stars." It looked just like the old sepia photographs, but with vivid colors like paintings. Appropriate, as Musson was travelling with a painter named Alberto Pisa, whose watercolors illustrated their subsequent travel book.

I tried to ignore the cranes in the new port, which were low enough not to be intrusive. In the old pictures one sees instead the masts of sailing ships and caïques with their graceful lateens punctuating the scene with white parentheses. Many of the vistas found in old photographs are gone, eradicated by modern buildings. It's a marvel when you can get a panorama comparable to those a century ago, or even forty years ago. But there's at least one reason not to feel too nostalgic about the earlier views of Monte Pellegrino. Nineteenth-century photographs show the mountain's slopes completely denuded. As early as 1791 Brian Hill noted that it was "a great barren mountain", though on the morning of February 4th he saw a very rare instance of its peaks covered in snow. Virtually all of Sicily was deforested by the middle of the sixteenth century, leading to soil erosion and the decline of agriculture. Now there are hundreds of thousands of trees, the result of twentieth-century planting campaigns and bans on grazing and logging.

Not quite as impressive as Cape Town's Table Mountain or Rio's Sugar Loaf Mountain, Monte Pellegrino is still spectacular. When Goethe saw it on the fresh spring day of April 2nd of 1787, he wrote that it was "the most beautiful headland in the world." Its cliffs are weathered into shades of gray and rust, its slopes clothed in green pines and cypresses. Its lower levels attract Palmeritani picnickers on the weekends, while the more devoted climb to the sacred cave-chapel of Santa Rosalia, the twelfth-century saint who delivered the city from the plague in 1624. In that year, as the city was in the grip of the Black Death, a man had a dream of a white dove that led him to Monte Pellegrino. When he awoke, he ascended the mountain and found Santa Rosalia's forgotten relics in the grotto that, centuries before, had been her hermit hideaway—relics so long neglected that the drops of mineralized water from the cave's roof had encased her body in a calcareous shell, literally incorporating her into the cavern's geology. The mummifying crust had to be broken away for her bones to be emancipated. Or so the legend goes. Released from their natural limestone sarcophagus, her relics were displayed through the boulevards of the beleaguered city, its atmosphere thick with the stench of putrefying corpses. It's thought that between May and December of 1624 ten-thousand people died. Eventually the plague lifted, Rosalia was credited with the city's deliverance, and ever since she's been Palermo's patron saint. It was high time the Palermitani finally committed, they'd been flirting with four other female saints through the years: Christina, Ninfa, Oliva, and Agatha. You can still find shrines to these saints who Rosalia superseded.

Subsequent to her salutary intercession Rosalia's bones lie in a giant silver sarcophagus, weighing 1400 pounds, in the Palermo cathedral. Cherubs frolic about its edges and the casket is brought out on her festival day, July 14th, in solemn pageant through the city's boulevards. She's the unofficial saint of biodiversity because the Yale zoologist G. E. Hutchison did his famous field research on water striders in ponds just below Santa Rosalia's cavern, thereby establishing Hutchinson's Ratio, a key evolutionary concept in biology. Many Palermitani parents name their girls Rosalia and her cave is reputed to be a refuge for lovers whose families don't approve of their union, thus ensuring her continued reputation with new generations for whom the menace of bubonic plague no longer holds compelling sway. More recently, fertility has become one of her side specialties and droves of women, eager to conceive, visit her shrine.

The plague had arrived in Palermo in the late spring of 1624, aboard a ship from Tunis. Within two months the *lazzaretto,* the quarantine hospital, was filled to overflowing. Carts came daily, laden with corpses. When Rosalia's relics were optimistically exhibited through Palermo's disease-ridden streets there was a young Flemish man in the crowd who had just arrived a few months before. His name was Anthony Van Dyck. He'd been commissioned to paint a portrait of the Spanish Viceroy Emanuele Filiberto of Savoy. Though only twenty-four years old, Van Dyck had already distinguished himself as one of Europe's premiere portrait artists, and the painting he did of the Viceroy is one of his masterpieces. Filiberto stands three-quarter length in his armor, with his helmet sporting an elaborate plume of feathers. He was forty years old at the sitting but his hairline had already receded. His armor is covered in an elaborate gilded decoration, while cuffs and collars of white ruffles make one wonder just how military the whole outfit was, more suggestive of a ballroom than a battlefield. Poor Filiberto didn't survive the pestilence that devastated his capital. Within months of having been immortalized by one of the greatest painters of all time he was dead. It's said that when the portrait was finished and hung in the palace it fell to the floor a few days later. Filiberto had rightly taken this to be a bad omen.

Van Dyck stayed only six months in Palermo during that desperate year, but his artistic experience was rich. On July 12th of 1624 he visited the famous painter Sofonisba Anguisola, one of the few women artists of the renaissance who had earned international fame in a man's profession. Van Dyck did a drawing of the ninety-six-year-old painter in his sketchbook. She's seated in a chair, bent over, with her frail arms barely holding her up. Surrounding the sketch Van Dyck penned his impressions. He noted that she was almost blind, but liked to have paintings put very close to her so she could make out details. All the more tragic, Van Dyck writes, because "her brain was still quick" and "her hand was still steady, without any tremor whatsoever." The greatest female painter of her age, Sofonisba Anguisola died three months after the young Flemish artist's visit. I was thinking of this when, after taking my pictures of Monte Pellegrino, I went to the church of San Giorgio dei Genovese, close to the old harbor. The interior is paved with tomb slabs commemorating Genoese traders who died in Palermo, including some relatives of Christopher Columbus. Sofonisba's simple tomb (she had married a Genoese merchant) is tucked in the top right corner, with a Latin epitaph that modestly notes her artistic accomplishments.

Another drawing by Van Dyck, made in that same year, offers us a fascinating glimpse into an aspect of Palermo's social world in the seventeenth century: a sketch of a woman in a tall conical hat who had been accused of witchcraft. Spain took control of Sicily in 1479 and the island was administered by a series of viceroys for centuries. The most tangible remains of this period can be found in the island's many Spanish baroque churches, but Van Dyck's drawing reminds us that Spain imported not only architectural styles but its Inquisition as well, and the witch, who the artist captured with a few elegant strokes of his crayon, is mute testament to the Spaniards' infamous fight against heresy. Detailed records were kept of these public trials and it so happens that there was only one prosecution during Van Dyck's stay, on May 19th of 1624 in the Piazza San Domenico, where six people were brought to the Inquisition's tribunal. You can visit this same piazza today and leisurely sip an espresso at the very spot the judgments took place. Leave a good tip should you be judged parsimonious. Four of the defendants were accused of bigamy, one was a blasphemer, and the last, the subject of Van Dyck's sketch, was the woman accused of witchcraft. All admitted their sins and begged forgiveness, which, documents tell us, was granted. Van Dyck depicted the woman as she carried a long candle, indicating her penitence. She still wears the peaked hat, decorated with a devil, which was put on her head to condemn her. Van Dyck's caption is succinct: *una strega in Palermo* ('a witch in Palermo'). In Sicily, some women accused of witchcraft were the so-called *donne di fuori* or 'women from the outside', who purportedly flew about and communed with fairies. They used their powers to heal people and do good things, but of course the religious authorities saw such folk superstitions differently.

By the time of Van Dyck's visit the Spanish Inquisition had been operating in Sicily for over a century. One of its most dramatic acts took place in 1492, a date American schoolchildren are taught to memorize because of Columbus's voyage; but it was also the year the Jews of Palermo were expelled from Sicily (and from all of Spain as well). In later years the Inquisition became even more vigorous in its quest to eradicate sacrilege. There's an engraving showing the mass trial of dozens of 'heretics' that took place on April 6th of 1724 in the large courtyard of the cathedral. Huge timber bleachers were constructed for the public proceedings. Travelers disembarking in Palermo's harbor could have their luggage searched for offending media, and the Inquisition would confiscate books if the content was thought to be perverse. Inquisitors policed every aspect of life, trying to mold the moral environment of the city. Homosexuality was thought to be particularly rife in Sicily. King Charles V believed it was the cause of Sicily's earthquakes and volcanic eruptions (in earlier centuries, for the same reasons, Peter of Blois thought Sicily was the entrance to hell). Only the richest citizens could pay their way out of punishment for homosexual acts, and the fees were higher than for murder. Those that couldn't bribe officials were burned alive in the special piazza set aside specifically for the execution of homosexuals. The Inquisitors confiscated the belongings of their victims, making the accusation of homosexuality a convenient way to get rid of a rival or raise a capital windfall. Inquisitors became very wealthy men. Officers were drawn from the nobility, who thus escaped condemnation for their sins and became even richer by punishing the perceived sins of others.

During Van Dyck's stay in Palermo he also did a painting envisioning the young Santa Rosalia, with long red hair, gazing heavenwards. She stands atop the rocky outcrop of Monte Pellegrino, with Palermo's harbor below. She points to the city, decimated by plague, pleading for God's mercy. Dark clouds have cast the city in the shadow of death, but the radiance on the saint's face indicates her intercession will succeed. It's almost as if Van Dyck had been summoned by fate to commit to canvas the visages of two of Palermo's most famous citizens, Filiberto and Sophonisba, just before they died; and give form to Rosalia, the saint who lifted the curse from the beleaguered city.

Monte Pellegrino offers a datum for anyone who might become disoriented in the streets of the old town, which twist and wander, but sometimes it's good to get lost; put the map in your pocket and trust in the fact that if you do get mislaid you can either (1) return to your map while sipping an espresso and make polite inquiries of the proprietor (those Italian lessons have to count for something) or, (2) wave down a taxi and give the driver the card from your hotel and a handful of banknotes. Either way you'll get back in one piece. I say this, but am myself an assiduous planner. I love maps, always have good ones, and scrutinize them before I head out for a day's sightseeing. I am at ease with the fact that in Italy a street sign is an occasional marker, sometimes very occasional. Many Italian streets also unpredictably change their designations, such as the one here in Palermo named after the Sicilian painter Giuseppe Sciuti, who gets only about a kilometer before the Via Restivo Empedocle takes over to the north and the Via Terra Santa picks up the baton to the south. Those two get even less than a kilometer before the name of the street changes yet again, which means in about two kilometers—a mile and a half—you could walk along a street that varies its name five times. This is irritating for Americans. Judging by that group of young Japanese tourists over there, each pointing in a different direction, it may be irritating to them too. We like a street to have one name along its entire length. Sensible, but one must give this up in Italy.

When Richard Payne Knight visited Palermo in 1777 he described the streets as "regular and clean" (though he found the architecture "extremely bad") but Johann Wolfgang von Goethe was Teutonically troubled by the thoroughfares just ten years later in 1787, finding them exasperatingly dirty and unhygienic. He even singled out Sicilian brooms for a design critique, noting, however, that even with good brooms little would have improved, since the shopkeepers, much to his annoyance, would sweep "everything into the middle of the street, which is, in consequence, so much the dirtier, and with every breath of wind send back to you the filth which has just before been swept into the roadway." Agitated, he queried a shop owner if "there was no board of regulations to prevent all of this." The merchant tells him, reasonably, that if they cleaned the streets then everyone would see how poorly they were paved, and, besides, the rich, who go about the town in their carriages, liked the spongy litter on the cobbles as it made their rides smoother.

Goethe had little good to say about Sicily or Sicilians. He reproved his local guide for recounting an ancient battle at a site at the edge of town, complaining that the "stupid guide" marred his enjoyment of nature "by his ill-timed erudition." A bit unfair since such information is exactly what one expects from guides even today. He judged Sicilian artworks to be mediocre and thought the nobility had provincial taste. There's one case where you can see if your opinions accord with Goethe's. He visited the Villa Palagonia, which survives today, not in Palermo proper but in Bagheria, about fifteen kilometers to the southeast. The villa's sculptural decorations consist of capriccios such as dwarfs, hybrid animals, half-animal/half-human figures, dragons and all kinds of imaginary monsters. Goethe hated the place: "This whole day has been taken up with the stupidities of the Prince Palagonia, …[he] gave free course to his humor and passion for the most ill-shapen and tasteless of erections. One would do him too much honor by giving him credit for even one spark of taste. The ugliness of these unshapely figures arranged without thought or purpose!" That's why the Via Goethe is a mere half kilometer long. If he'd been nicer he might've got a lengthier stretch. He did like Palermo's public gardens, though, especially the Villa Giulia and Botanical Gardens. He claims to have "passed some most delightful hours" in them, and fondly noted that those "wonderful gardens have made a deep and lasting impression on my mind."

Unhappily, today, even though the main roads are kept very clean, one steps off the beaten path and finds debris in the streets. As one Palermitan graffiti artist has scrawled above a phalanx of overflowing dumpsters: "In Trash We Trust." Still, when Guy de Maupassant visited Palermo in the spring of 1885 he found those less than perfect alleys picturesque and interesting, noting that, "the streets of Palermo are ... wide and beautiful in the wealthy quarters; in the poor sections they resemble the colourful lanes of oriental towns." Litter aside, I'd say that was still true. Yet there are little urban tragedies tucked away everywhere in Palermo, where past greatness has turned through time to dereliction. One is the Piazza Lolli, overseen by the magnificent but now completely dilapidated Lolli train station. It was built in 1891, at the height of Palermo's fortunes. In front of the station the piazza is strewn with beer bottles and the charred remains of fires that the homeless light. Only vagrants and surreptitious teenagers visit it, yet one envisions a wonderful green space and the station restored to its former glory. The Piazza Lolli is still nobly overseen by the bronze statue of an 18th century poet from nearby Cinisi, Giovanni Meli. Perhaps it's appropriate that Meli's statue holds court here, accompanying the vagrants, since one of his poems reads:

...Disguised, he roams at night
Hiding in any nook and cranny;
He enjoys the company of vagabonds...
Since he remains a true friend
To all who are bizarre, capricious and bold.

The Corso Vittorio Emanuele is a wide avenue that runs, you'll be relieved to know, a good two kilometers from *La Cala* to a monumental city gate that no visitor to Palermo should miss, the Porta Nuova, through which the aforementioned Corso passes, and where the name of the street changes to Corso Calatafimi, just in case you were feeling complacent. The Corso Vittorio Emanuele and the Via Maqueda (the latter named after the Spanish Viceroy of Sicily 1598-1601, Bernardino de Cárdenas y Portugal Duque de Maqueda—aren't you glad they didn't use his full name?) are Palermo's most important streets, intersecting at the Quattro Canti or 'Four Corners' with its four fountains, a terrific monument begun in 1608 by Giulio Lasso. An English traveler, Patrick Brydone, visited this very crossing—though he calls it the *Ottangolo* or 'Octagon'—and wrote a letter about it to a friend in London on June 23rd of 1770, in which he described it as "adorned with elegant buildings." He says that from the square you can see "the whole of these noble streets, and the four great gates of the city that terminate them; the symmetry and beauty of which produce a fine effect." He also mentions that he's heard that the main streets will soon have lamps lighting them, which he anticipates will "be the finest sight in the world." For contemporary tourists, too, this is the city's center, but as Brydone indicates it's been Palermo's heart for centuries and marked the intersection of the four main quadrants or *mandamenti* of the city which the

Spanish codified in the 17th century: the Kalsa quarter in the southeast, the Albergheria quarter in the southwest, the Loggia quarter in the northeast, and the Seralcadi quarter in the northwest.[1]

The Quattro Canti's structures are like four compass points with their facades hierarchically arranged. At the lower levels, just above the four fountains that symbolize the city's four ancient rivers, are allegorical figures of the four seasons, while on the next tiers are statues of four Spanish kings who ruled Sicily during the sixteenth and seventeenth centuries: Charles V (r. 1516-56), Philip II (r. 1556-98; also known as 'Philip the Prudent', although in 1588 he imprudently sent the Spanish Armada to invade England; less than a third of his ships returned), Philip III (r. 1598-1621; during whose reign the Quattro Canti were made), and Philip IV (r. 1621-65). At the apex of each quadrant are the four early female saints who Santa Rosalia superseded and who were given suzerainty over their respective quarters: Agatha (Kalsa), Cristina of Bolsena (Albergheria), Olivia (Loggia) and Ninfa (Seralcadi).

There's nowhere to sit at the Quattro Canti, so there are always tourists standing below one of the four facades and looking up at the others, taking snapshots. It's a favorite hangout for the chaps who drive horse-drawn carriages and who troll for fares in the shady angles of the piazza. They've been around for centuries. Joseph Hager, who stayed several months in Palermo in 1796, noted of these carriages that, "as the horse may be managed by a single person, they are of great utility; for, by means of them one may go from one extremity of the city to the other with wonderful speed, nay, almost fly." It's still true today. I've seen them race along at breakneck speeds. In the mid-nineteenth century drainage at the Quattro Canti was apparently a problem. In 1840, when the English traveler Arthur John Strutt went for a walk after a night of heavy rain, he wrote in his travel diary that the Quattro Canti flooded and they had to build elevated wooden walkways for pedestrians.

While the intersection might not seem geographically central today, especially when you look at a modern map, it was perfectly central to the medieval, renaissance, and baroque cities. In older maps of Palermo, even one as late as 1893, you can see it clearly; the circular piazza is like a target in the center, right in the crosshairs of the Vittorio Emanuele and Maqueda. So vital are these two streets to the life of Palermo that they are affectionately and simply known as *Il Corso* and *La Via,* first among the boulevards, a masculine and a feminine juncture at the heart of the city. But Il Corso / Vittorio Emanuele is also frequently referred to as Il Cassaro, a corruption of its Arabic name, derived from *Al Qasara,* or 'The Castle', a structure to which the street led in the Muslim era. Just to make your head spin, the same street was known during Spanish rule as the Via Toledo.

The Porta Nuova, the city gate at the west end of Il Corso, is an arch in the genus of the old triumphal arches of the ancient Roman emperors, who many later European rulers tried to emulate, often, as here, maladroitly. The portal was first built in the sixteenth century by King Charles I of Spain (r. 1516-1556; bewilderingly, better known as Charles V, Holy Roman Emperor, a title he also had from 1519-1556) to commemorate a victory over the Ottoman Turks. The first version of the arch was blown up when a gunpowder magazine exploded. It was reconstructed in its present form in 1669. Old engravings show processions passing through the gate and a large parade ground beside it (now the Piazza del Parlamento), with festive banners flying from the arch's peaks. Its most remarkable features are giant sculptures depicting defeated Turks, who have turbans and serpentine moustaches like the bad guys in old movies. Two have had their arms chopped off, as if to warn prospective aggressors. This grisly sight is a macabre celebration of Charles' taking of the city of Tunis from the Ottomans in 1535. It's hardly something he should have been proud of. His army slaughtered 30,000 people when they pillaged the city, including Christians, Jews, and Muslims, and his armada had been financed by gold paid by the Inca to liberate their captured king, Atahualpa, who, even after the ransom was paid, was executed.

Islam had penetrated well into the Mediterranean at an early date. By the late eighth century Muslims had conquered the Middle East, all of North Africa as well as most of Spain. There was as much Muslim Mediterranean coastline as there was Christian, and Islam would only increase its ratio in the coming centuries as the Ottoman Empire superseded the Byzantine and expanded their territories west, in the sixteenth century twice laying siege to Vienna and controlling several European countries such as Hungary, Albania, Greece, Croatia, Serbia, and other Balkan states. It was only in the later sixteenth century that the Ottoman Empire slowly began to contract, but it took another four hundred years before it came to an end after World War I.

The Muslims conquered Sicily in 831 CE and ruled the island for almost two-hundred and fifty years. Not a lot is known about this period. An Arab traveler named Ibn al-Atir wrote that when the Muslims took Palermo from the Byzantines it was a terrible slaughter and the population went from 70,000 to 3,000. Still, later visitors saw a bustling city with a thriving economy. The Normans subjugated the island in the 1070s and ruled for a brief but brilliant hundred and fifty year period, leaving a rich heritage of art and architecture. The Normans who captured Sicily (I am haunted by a Monty Pythonesque scenario of an army made up entirely of soldiers named Norman) were a branch of the same family who, at about the same time, subjugated England. The Norman invader William the Conqueror captured England from the Saxons in 1066 at the

Battle of Hastings, an event uniquely memorialized in that singular piece of needlework, the Bayeux Tapestry. In this same year the brothers Robert Guiscard ('The Cunning') and Roger I (apparently 'Not As Cunning') were consolidating territories in Sicily, taking Palermo in 1072, Trapani in 1077, Taormina in 1079, and Catania in 1081; but Sicily was not completely conquered until 1091, and it was not made officially a Norman kingdom until the 1130s, with Roger II (r. 1139-1154) the first king of the realm.

I contemplate this rich history when I walk Palermo's streets. There seems to be the full range of Mediterranean visages strolling past: Africans, Arabs, Greeks, Italians, Norsemen ... the list is potentially endless. I saw a man with a dark complexion and black hair, short-cropped and curly, wearing a silk business suit, talking on his cell phone while sipping a macchiato; then, turning a corner there was a chestnut-haired woman with icy blue eyes and skin an ethereal white preparing her shop's window display; genetic codes from Africa to Scandinavia in the space of a few strides, as if this city in the center of the Mediterranean had become a minestrone of the DNA of everyone who had ever conquered it. Myriad genes wind through the streets of the city, its history twinkling in the eyes of its citizens. Recent years have brought even more immigration: Tamils from Sri Lanka, Bangladeshis, Indians, Muslims from Tunisia and Libya, and Africans from Eritrea, Nigeria, and various other countries. It's hard to imagine a more polyglot city, as if it was the nexus of the world. Modern Palermo celebrates its varied faces, or at least some people do, and while you can admire the art and architecture of the city, don't forget to look at those faces and smile, to be rewarded in kind, one of travel's most satisfying and affirming recompenses.

The Porta Nuova is just a short walk to the medieval palace, which was begun by the Normans in the late 11th century but was renovated throughout history, parts of it functioning today as the Sicilian regional parliament. But the Normans weren't the first on the block. The Arabs had a palace there before them, and remains from the Phoenician period have been uncovered at the lowest levels. So it's been a busy place for about 2200 years. Today as well, since the Palatine Chapel, built by the Norman king Roger II in 1132, attracts tens of thousands of visitors a year.

Contemporary historians celebrate how the Norman kings reigned over a society known for ethnic and religious tolerance. In the 12th and 13th centuries Roger II and his heirs utilized both Muslims and Greeks in various parts of their bureaucracies. They used Muslims as sailors and soldiers, and during Roger II's reign a Greek, George of Antioch, was raised to the most important office of the realm, *Amir* (or *Ammiraglio*). Christian abbots even permitted their serfs to swear fealty on the Koran rather than the Bible. But Roger's laws indicate that Catholicism was still the favored religion, and Roger seems to have become less inclusive as he grew older. The chronicler Romuald of Salerno wrote that, "towards the end of his life, allowing secular matters to be neglected and delayed, he labored in every conceivable way to convert Jews and Muslims to the faith of Christ, and endowed converts with many gifts and resources." Roger's doubts about his own salvation became keener, perhaps, as he approached death. This led to a sad moment in the history of his reign: the December 1153 execution of Philip of Mahdiyya, who had been raised in Roger's court. Philip seems to have secretly remained Muslim even though he'd outwardly shifted religious allegiances and declared himself Christian. Roger was furious at the duplicity and had Philip dragged through the streets by horses and then burned alive.

Whatever the fantasies about ethnic equality during Norman rule the fact was that Jews, Muslims and Greek Orthodox Christians didn't have the same status as Catholics. Ibn Jubayr tells of a jurist, Ibn Zur'a, who converted to Christianity, presumably for economic rather than religious reasons. It's likely that many Muslims converted to Christianity simply to make their lives easier and to avoid higher taxes. Earlier, when the Muslims conquered Sicily around 830, many Christian inhabitants converted to Islam for the very same reasons that the Muslims 230 years later would convert to Christianity. This see-sawing led to hybrid beliefs. When the Arab traveler Ibn Hawqal visited Sicily in 973 he complained about Muslims who didn't follow the precepts of Islam and whose sons married Muslims but whose daughters married Christians, as if the two religions were strangely merged: "Most people are bastardised Muslims and think it is acceptable to marry Christians on the basis that their male child follows the father by being a bastardised Muslim, while the female child becomes a Christian like her mother. They do not pray, do not perform ritual ablutions, they do not pay the alms tax nor do they go on pilgrimage to Mecca."

In language, too, the cultures seemed to have intertwined, with many Orthodox Christians fluent in both Arabic and their mother tongue, Greek; and Jews who could shuttle between Hebrew and the island's other predominant languages, making them invaluable as translators for business transactions. Elsewhere, Ibn Hawqal was appalled by the immorality of the Sicilian Muslims. He wrote that the towns of the coast were "packed with hypocrisy, dissimulation, the unemployed and the godless who are all trouble-makers." He thought the people "complete disasters." Many of them, he noted, "act as pimps; and there are some among them who do not consider it particularly hypocritical, but reputable."

A couple of centuries after Ibn Hawqal's visit, Roger II's grandson, King William II (r. 1166-1189) presided over a Sicily that retained a significant

Muslim population despite having been conquered by Christians a century before. Ibn Jubayr, a Muslim pilgrim, made many observations about the lives of Muslims in Sicily when he visited the island in 1184. He noted of William II that "the attitude of the King is truly extraordinary. He has a perfect conduct towards the Muslims; he gives them employment; he chooses his officers among them, and all, or almost all, keep their faith secret and remain attached to the beliefs of Islam. The king has full faith in Muslim subjects … to the extent that the head of his kitchens is a Muslim." At the same time some Muslims felt restricted by their circumstances. When Ibn Jubayr visited a fellow Muslim named Abd al-Massih, the latter grumbled, "You can boldly display your faith in Islam… but we must conceal our faith, and, fearful of our lives, must … discharge of our religious duties in secret. We are bound in the possession of an infidel (the Christians) who has placed on our necks the noose of bondage." So at least one Muslim didn't think it was an equal society. Yet Ibn Jubayr's own impressions seem to counter al-Massih's complaint. He writes that Sicily is "filled with worshippers of the cross … the Muslims live beside them with their property and their farms. The Christians treat these Muslims well and have taken them to themselves as friends." Having noted this, however, he also observes that Christians "impose on them a tax to be paid twice yearly, thus taking from them the amplitude of living they had been wont to earn from that land." He may have owed his life to William. Ibn Jubayr's ship had run aground in a storm near Messina, and he later learned that the king personally paid for the boats to rescue the passengers and crew.

Ibn Jubayr tells an interesting tale, told to him by Yahya ibn Fityan, the royal court embroiderer, fascinating if really true. He writes that the handmaids of the noblewomen of the royal court were all Muslims, and that they had successfully converted the Christian ladies in waiting to Islam, which of course was hidden from the king and other noblemen. When an earthquake struck, and from the women's quarters calls for the mercy of Allah reso nated through the palace, the charade was exposed. King William was said to have shrugged his shoulders, saying "Let each invoke the God he worships."

Ibn Jubayr had time for girl-watching while in Palermo and noted that the Christian women dressed like their Muslim counterparts: "The finery of the Christian women is that of Muslim women. They are clad in fabrics of silk embroidered with gold, draped in magnificent robes, covered with veils of many colours; they wear all the finery of Muslim women, including powders and perfumes."

Despite relative tolerance the trend was to purge the island of Muslims. When Robert Guiscard and Roger I conquered Palermo in early January of 1072 it had been an Islamic city for 230 years, and while the Norman overlords may have kept many Muslims employed and given them some protections and freedom of worship, their status on the island steadily degraded over the decades, leading finally—between 1224 and 1246—to Muslim minority unrest, resulting in their mass deportation to a depopulated town in Apulia called Lucera where Emperor Frederick II used them to revive the local economy. The town came to be known as *Lucceria Sarracenorum,* or 'Lucera of the Saracens' reflecting the new ethnic makeup. This colony survived only seventy-five years until its members were driven away to Albania or captured and sold into slavery. Such was the fate of the last Sicilian Muslims.

The Jews of Palermo experienced a similar degradation of their numbers, though there had been far fewer Jews than Muslims. As in other cities of the Mediterranean Jews had to wear badges to identify themselves. Christians were not the only people to impose this upon an ethnic group. When the Muslims gained control of Sicily they made Jews wear a badge of a monkey and Christians wear a badge of a pig. When the Jewish traveler Benjamin of Tudela visited the island in 1170, he noted that there were 1500 Jews in Palermo. When the Jews were expelled from the island in 1492 they numbered about 5000 persons in Palermo alone—one fifth of the city's estimated total population of 25,000—and their eviction made the Catholicization of Sicily complete.

A few years ago, working on a small cruise ship, I arrived in Palermo just after the Arab Spring revolts in Tunisia in 2011. The ferry from Tunis had docked just hours before, filled with young men wanting to use Palermo as a hopping off point for employment in Europe. But the immigration police had stopped them from disembarking and were sending them back. There must have been two or three hundred of them, all lined along the railings at the stern of the ship, looking out and almost close enough to touch the city, but still a world away. Some were laughing, making the best of it, while others had a thousand-yard stare, as if they were wondering what kind of future they might have—Muslims trying to get back into Sicily eight centuries after their expulsion.

One of the ways to learn about medieval Sicilian society is to look at the laws promulgated by Roger II in the early twelfth century. They provide a window onto a fascinating social order. Criminals who found refuge in a church were not allowed to be forcibly removed, unless they were from the lowest class (serfs) and had stolen their master's property, in which case they could be dragged out screaming. Nobody was allowed to sell or barter in holy relics (bones of saints), supposedly because there were so many fakes and the faithful could easily be taken advantage of. An old goat's bone, properly curated, could be passed off by a persuasive salesman as a tibia of St Francis.[2] In medieval Palermo the rape of a nun brought the death penalty, as did forging a royal seal or altering a royal letter, but if you were a jester and just dressed up like a nun for a laugh you were merely flogged in public. Those who forged or clipped the metal from a coin of the realm were deprived of their lives and property.

The laws concerning adultery were complex, as if this was the chief social problem. Women who committed it had their noses slashed, so their sin was ever visible, unless the wronged husband objected to the mutilation, in which case flogging could be substituted. Nose slitting, too, was the punishment for mothers who pimped out their virgin daughters, but if the daughters became prostitutes of their own free will the mother wasn't held responsible. A husband who discovered his wife *in flagrante* with her lover could kill both with no penalty, though he had to do it right away, that is, in the heat of the moment. Prostitutes, however, were "absolutely immune" from punishment for adultery or fornication because, simply put, it was their profession. They were not to associate with women "of good reputation", however, so as to avoid confusion.

It was lunchtime so I went to a bakery and bought a couple of fresh *panini*, then to a grocer's where I got some cheese, slices of salami and a lunch-box-size carton of grape juice, the ones with the bendy straw in a piece of cellophane glued to the box; the ones that, if you grasp them too hard the purple juice spurts up the straw and all over your white shirt bought new for this trip. The upside to this was the amusement of two pretty schoolgirls in private school regalia who had taken up a bench next to me in the piazza beside the magnificent Norman-era cathedral. Having had the considerable foresight to pack an OxyClean gel stick (NB: Saint Clare of Assisi is the patron saint of launderers), I could share in their laughter and enjoy my sandwiches despite the Jackson Pollock decoration on my shirt. The benches were covered with graffiti, mostly of the predictable 'Guido loves Maria' variety, scribbled with silvery felt pens. As if on cue two boys, also emblazoned with aristocratic school patches, joined the two girls and they shuffled to cozier angles. I went back to the Excelsior—a good post-prandial walk—showered, read for a bit, and set my alarm for one hour later.

Afternoon

Revived in the Mediterranean manner I set out once again. From the Excelsior it was a pleasant walk along the Via Libertà before I got to the conjoined Piazzas Castelnuovo and Ruggiero Settimo, the latter dramatically overseen by the monumental arch of the nineteenth-century Teatro Politeama Garibaldi, once home to Palermo's symphony orchestra and a host to stage performances. Atop are huge bronze sculptures of Apollo with Euterpe, the muse of music and lyric poetry, in a chariot. I took out my handy pocket binoculars to get a better look. They're wonderful, with the horses rearing up in all directions, like something you'd imagine on the buildings of ancient

Rome. There's a gallery with wall paintings done in a Pompeii style, imitating frescoes discovered at the ancient city buried by the eruption of Vesuvius. Elegant figures in Roman dress dance about, to the music in the theater, I guess. As I walked around the building I started to appreciate the building's exuberant embodiment of the Neoclassical style. Some of the ironwork, such as the lantern posts, is as good as anything you can see in Paris. Ruggiero Settimo's marble statue stands in the eponymous piazza, and I sat down for a bit while he stood guard over me.

Ignominious blobs of pigeon droppings ran down his temple. He was from a Sicilian noble family and had a career as navy commander, politician, revolutionary, and even the head of state for the brief sixteen-month period of Sicilian independence in 1848-49. When that hopeful moment ended, Settimo fled to Malta to live in exile. Not such a bad fate.

The Via della Libertà, compelled by Ruggiero's stern glare, changes its name to the Via Ruggiero Settimo here at the piazza, and if you thought that Palermo had thrown its best pitch in terms of theaters, you're in for a curveball in five hundred meters, where in the Piazza Verdi the even more monumental Teatro Massimo holds court. And *massimo* it certainly is, by some accounts the third largest theater in Europe. It's hard to believe that this wonderful building lay derelict for over twenty years before it became the centerpiece of Palermo's urban revitalization plans in the 1990s. When it did reopen, Hillary Clinton gave a speech in it on the importance of civic education for young people. It's main entrance staircase is more famous, however, for providing the monumental backdrop for the shooting of Michael Corleone and the killing of his daughter (played by Sofia Coppola) at the end of *The Godfather Part III* as the beautiful intermezzo from Mascangi's *Cavalleria rusticana* plays with multiple tones of irony over the tragedy and, ultimately, Michael's death. Of the many ironies, not the least is that the mafia-controlled Palermo construction companies wanted to demolish the theater, the cultural centerpiece of the old town.[3] Overhead, just below the pediment, is an inscription: L'ARTE RENNOVA I POPOLI E NE RIVELA LA VITA ["Art renews the people and reveals their life"] and underneath: VANNO DELLE SCENE IL DILETTO OVE NON MIRI A PREPARAR L'AVVENIRE ["Enjoying the scenes is useless unless it prepares us for the future"]. They're appropriate words. No building in Palermo represents the city's hopefulness more eloquently.

For the moment, though, I'd reached my daily limit of Neoclassicism, so I decided to go for some real classicism at the archaeological museum in the Piazza dell'Olivella. The museum is a bit dowdy. Long ago, the building was the convent of the Chiesa dell'Olivella, but now it has a once-grand-but-now-underfunded look, though the fellow at the ticket counter told me there's a major renovation planned. Edward Hutton, an American traveler who visited around 1925, wasn't impressed by the museum's curatorial department. He found the artefacts displayed in "a marvelous confusion, due to the unsuitable building, an extraordinary collection of beautiful and banal objects." When he got to the Greek sculptures, however, he was mollified and much happier, as any sane person would be.

I have a rule for museums, though, like many rules I make for myself, I often find excuses to break them. The idea is not to feel obliged to see everything. Nothing can dull your appreciation of art like an overdose of it. And since art is potent stuff, it doesn't take much. Today, I just wanted to see the sculptures from the ancient Greek temples at Selinunte, the artifacts the museum is most famous for. I wasn't disappointed; they were spectacular. They were carved in limestone, but sometimes the faces or hands of the figures were done in white marble and then attached to the main part of the bodies. One of the best is in the scene of Diana (Artemis) calmly setting Actaeon's own hunting dogs on him as she changes him into a stag as punishment for accidently seeing her emerge naked from her bath. Diana's face and arms are done in marble, while the rest of her is in the coarser stone, as if the patrons of the temple tried to balance their worry that she might be angered by being duplicated in a base material with the expense of the marble. The Selinunteans fudged on the marble and, alas, their city was destroyed. That's what you get for short-changing a spiteful goddess.

There's also a remarkable bronze ram in the museum. It's life size and was found in Syracuse, in the southeast corner of Sicily. It's preternaturally realistic. One almost expects it to bleat, lower its head and charge the ample bum of that woman over there taking a selfie in front of a Grecian urn. One can only hope. I'd never seen anything quite like it before. Was it a votive offering to a god; a ram for bloodless sacrifice ever reclining on the temple's steps? Its blank stare reminded me of the figures of the recumbent bull, Nandi, at Shiva temples in India.

My hour limit at the museum was approaching but there was one more object I wanted to see; a four-thousand year-old Egyptian stele covered in hieroglyphics called the Palermo Stone. Oddly, there's a hip-hop singer from Pittsburg who has adopted this as his stage name. No, I haven't a clue, but I suspect it doesn't have anything to do with a keen interest in Egyptian archaeology of the First Dynasty (ca. 3200 to 3000 BCE). The Palermo Stone is one of seven known fragments of what was a single large slab with inscriptions listing the deeds of the early Egyptian pharaohs. Some parts are in Cairo, another is in London. The Palermo section of this scattered artefact was bought by a Sicilian lawyer in the middle of the nineteenth century and has been in the museum's collection since 1877. Nobody was looking at it and it seemed rather lonely and, like too many things in this museum, not displayed in its best light. In some respects it resembles a more famous but much younger cousin—only two thousand years old—the Rosetta Stone, the trilingual decree in Egyptian, Greek, and Demotic in the British Museum. I looked around to see if anyone else appreciated this neglected gem, but there was nary a tourist or bored museum guard to be found. I glanced at my watch just as my hour was up.

Emerging into the sunlight I took a moment to contemplate the beautiful but decayed baroque façade of the church beside the museum, the Chiesa di San Ignazio all' Olivella, built between 1598 and 1622, though the dome was not completed until 1732. It's a pretty church, among the nicer of Palermo's many baroque masterpieces. I went in and sat on the pews and, as the organist rehearsed the wedding march, recalled dramatic pictures I'd seen of this church after the Allied bombings of 1943. The entire roof and dome was gone and the nave was filled with an enormous mountain of rubble from the collapsed vaulting. All of what I was looking up at was post World War II reconstruction.

Despite having slept well I started to feel jet lag creeping up on me so I went to the Ballerò Market, sometimes called the Arab Market, to generate some fresh energy. Everyone likes open air markets in foreign countries because we get our over-packaged food from inauthentic supermarkets contaminated with Muzak. In Palermo's markets you can still hear the cries of the fish mongers, fruit sellers, vegetable vendors and the cheese merchants all noisily vying for your business; a sound out of the middle ages in a terrific cacophony of commerce. Somehow a bright jumble of oranges in a Sicilian open air market is more compelling, and photogenic, than a carefully arranged pyramid of clones in the Franken-fruit section of Albertsons. It's the same with laundry, apparently, because I always see tourists taking pictures of it, as if hanging clothes on a line is some quaint thing from another time. I was once in Naples and some lingerie was swaying on a balcony. Below, a gaggle of middle-aged male tourists wearing khaki travel vests and Tilley hats collided with one another, surreptitiously taking pictures. They got their comeuppance presently when a muscular young man wearing only tight cutoff jeans appeared on the balcony and plucked the lacy fruits from the vine, looked down, and threw that muddled flock of slack-jawed seniors a cheerful kiss, much to the amusement of their wives who, no doubt, torture their husbands with that incident to this very day.

The Ballerò Market was in medieval times the Greek quarter of the city and it's still one of the most pleasant areas to explore. I spent an hour wandering through the stalls, bought some blood oranges, and talked to some Australians whose tour bus had regurgitated them into the market's labyrinth for a half hour scurry through. They were desperately hankering for a cold beer, as Australians do. I cheerfully recommended having a fresh orange instead, holding one of mine triumphantly aloft, and in unison they directed towards me a scornful glower I won't attempt to describe. While we're on markets, another good one is the famous Mercato della Vucciria just south of the Piazza San Domenico, where heretics used to be burned. There was once a prison there, and the wives of the prisoners set up their fruit and vegetable stalls below their husbands' cells, probably so they could send and receive messages on strings, or send up contraband or gifts to make prison life easier. The Mercato delle Pulci (literally, 'flea market') is the market for antiques and collectibles. It stems off of the Piazza Papireto—named after the river that once flowed there—just a few meters northwest of the cathedral.

I came out of the Ballerò near the train station and walked into the square in front of it. In a regrettable quirk of negligent town planning—one might say cavalier—it's an unfortunate fact that as one emerges from the Palermo train station into the Piazza Giulio Cesare one is greeted by a horse's anus. That welcoming—yet at the same time offending—orifice belongs to the equine portion of a monumental bronze statue of Garibaldi. Just to the north there's a pair of buildings creating a gateway to the Via Roma, one of the city's main thoroughfares. These buildings might seem like old baroque structures until you realize they're devoid of any exuberance, as if the style has been wrung out of them.

They're examples of Fascist architecture with eagles gracing the tops of the two towers. As far as Fascist architecture goes, these are less severe than many specimens of the genre, and at least give a nod to the city's architectural past. There are some good examples of Fascist architecture in Palermo, from the era overseen by *Il Duce* ('The Duke"), Benito Mussolini, Italy's dictator from 1925 to 1943.

Looking at my map I realized that while I was in this part of the city I should see two things on my checklist. The first was the Bridge of the Admiral (c. 1130), built by one of medieval Palermo's most fascinating figures, George of Antioch, the *Amir* or governor for Roger II, the commander of his navy, and patron of one of Palermo's most beautiful churches, the Martorana.[4] The second was Palermo's first Norman-era church, San Giovanni dei Lebbrosi or St John of the Lepers.

It was an easy walk from the train station to the bridge. The Bridge of the Admiral is preserved in a little park, at an angle that shows how canalization has redirected the natural course of the Oreto River, which is now constrained by an unattractive concrete sluice. The elegant span is now exiled seventy meters from the watercourse it once forded. There was a teenage couple sitting in the park and the boy was trying his darnedest to kiss the girl, but she always managed to avert her lips at the last moment and so he kept missing the target, getting a mouthful of hair or a sweaty temple for his efforts. The entire time I was there he never let up, even while she maintained a successful run of evasions.

The Bridge of the Admiral was on the main road from Palermo to Cefalù and, eventually, Messina, the hopping-off point for the toe of Italy. I couldn't help but wonder what this bridge would've looked like when it was built in the early twelfth century. This area would have been idyllic countryside, well beyond the ramparts of the town. Farms would have surrounded the Oreto's banks, drawing its waters for crops. I tried to imagine the pastoral scene eight centuries ago with the sparkling river winding gently under the bridge's arches, its shores green with spring grass and dappled with wildflowers. A shepherd with his bleating charges regards me from a hillock; a creaking cart, drawn by a tired horse and attended by an old peasant couple, shrugs over the bridge's crest. My bucolic fantasy might be entirely romantic. The Arab historian Abu Abdullah al-Idrisi, a member of Roger II's court in the 1140s, noted that the Oreto powered "a very large number of mills that suffice for the needs of the town." Still, there's an eighteenth-century engraving that echoes my rural vision. Goethe's letter of Wednesday April 4th, 1787 also suggests a pastoral landscape: "In the afternoon we paid a visit to the fertile and delightful valley … through which the Oreto meanders … and was shaded by a lovely group of trees, behind which an uninterrupted prospect opened up the valley, affording a view of several farm buildings."

It was a short walk from the bridge to San Giovanni dei Lebbrosi, which gets its name from the lepers' hospital that was once attached to it. Legend has it that Robert Guiscard had this church built in 1072 as his army had been encamped here for the siege of Palermo. Here, too, one struggles to imagine a scene from long ago amongst the urban sprawl. Although the other Norman churches such as the Martorana and San Giovanni degli Eremiti are more famous, I love this little building. It doesn't have any fancy mosaics or famous frescoes but I like its simplicity and quiet grandeur. As I approached the door three elderly people were emerging, a portly woman all in black held the key, and she muttered "chiuso". I pleaded in my best Italian for a few minutes to take pictures. She nodded her consent and walked with the couple to the street. I enjoyed being alone for a while, sitting in the pews and appreciating the peacefulness. Owing to the church's obscurity, there were no tourists. An old man came in, swaddled in a dark, dusty jacket. He crossed himself with a quivering hand. He stood in front of the altar in silence for a moment then drifted away. It was a scene of quiet devotion of a type reenacted here for over a thousand years. As I left I put some coins in the paper cup of a man who was begging near the church's entrance, buoyed by the caretaker's generosity in letting me in at closing time.

I was tired, but a quick sandwich and *café coretto* at a small *panificio* gave me the energy for a walk to the remains of the Favara palace, also known as *Maredolce* (or *Castello de Mar Dolce*). It was the largest of all the countryside villas of the Norman kings, built by Roger II in 1153. It derives its name from the Arabic *fawwara,* meaning a spring of fresh water. The palace and its grounds must have been extensive. Romuald of Salerno described it, and it's worth getting his full account: "[Roger] created a pleasure garden at a place which was called Favara, with many canals and streams, into which he ordered different types of fish, brought from many different regions ... He had some of the hills and woods around about Palermo enclosed with a stone wall, and ordered a delightful and well-stocked park made, planted with all sorts of trees, and in it he had deer, roebucks and wild boars kept. And he had a palace in this part to which he ordered water to be brought by underground pipes from the clearest of springs. So this wise and careful man enjoyed these aforesaid pleasures as the nature of the season suggested; for in winter, and in Lent because of its profusion of fish, he dwelled at the Favara palace; while in the summer he made the fiery season's heat bearable at the Parco, and diverted his mind from his many cares and the strain of his duties by a moderate amount of hunting."

Today the remnants of Favara are surrounded by modern buildings on one side and open to orchards in the south. A swampy depression indicates where the palace's lake used to be. In fact, a medieval Arab traveler implies that the palace was on an island in the midst of an artificial reservoir. The Arab poet Abdurahman, who probably never actually saw the building, waxed poetic about Favara: "O how beautiful is the lakelet of the twin palm trees and the island where the spacious palace stands! The clear waters of the double springs are like liquid pearls!" I tried to imagine a delightful garden around that uninspiring puddle, but my imagination was faltering and I knew my body's clock was not yet tuned to Sicilian time. I dragged myself to the train station and took the bus back into the comforting arms of the Excelsior. I took a hot shower, collapsed in my bed, and slept soundly for eleven hours.

DAY TWO

The first of these towns [of Sicily] is Palermo, a city that is both most remarkable for its grandeur and most illustrious for its importance... It is endowed with qualities that confer upon it an unequalled glory and combine beauty and nobility... endowed with magnificent buildings, which welcome travelers and flaunt the beauty of their construction, the skill of their design and their marvelous originality.

–Al-Idrisi, *The Book of Roger,* 1154

Morning

The breakfast at the Excelsior, including strong coffee, fortified me for a day of urban exploration. I decided to sever the umbilicus of the Via della Libertà and wander the narrow back streets to the cathedral, which is best visited in the late morning when the sun illuminates the expansive south side of the church. It was 9:00 am and the light was lucid in the way that only Mediterranean light can be. I soon saw the cathedral's dome and made my way over to the same piazza where I'd sprayed my shirt with grape juice the day before. The Palermo cathedral is a festive, wedding cake of a structure adorned by its Norman and Arab past, but altered by later additions. In former times, the people of the city referred to it as *Matrice,* or Mother

Church. The dome was added in the seventeenth century, plunked down atop the original medieval structure. Most people decry this addition, but I think the architect did a decent job integrating it. The British traveler A. J. Strutt passed through Palermo in 1840 and wrote that "the rich ensemble of gothic architecture is strangely spoilt by the modern addition of a new Roman cupola, very white and clean." The white limestone, however, has weathered since Strutt's visit and now matches the color of the rest of the church.

The south entrance has an imposing triple-arched portico. There's a pediment above with a sculpture of Christ enthroned in the center, raising his hand in blessing. On either side are arrayed the *dramatis personae* of the Annunciation: on the left the archangel Gabriel, his 'announcement' in medieval Latin unfurling on a banner flying in front of him, and on the right the Virgin Mary. Mary's lectern holds the Old Testament she was supposedly reading at the time of Gabriel's arrival. The book's tilted towards you, as if the artist couldn't quite figure out the perspective. In front of the Virgin is a vase with a gangly stalk of lilies, symbols of her purity, so tall and top-heavy one expects it to fall over. Above are flying angels, one playing a harp and the other strumming what might be the ancestor of the modern guitar, which made its appearance in the twelfth century, just when the cathedral was being built. Both Gabriel and Mary are rigidly posed, even though the sculptor suggested motion in the drapery of the alighting archangel. Gabriel's head is oddly shaped, like a wedge, and he frowns, with his mouth slightly open. He stares back at you, as if he's surprised and a bit put off that you've appeared out of nowhere and are taking his picture. Mary's hands stick out like appendages for a Mr. Potato Head. Around everything curls spiraling Gothic tracery. Below is a row of enthroned Christian saints, their rank punctuated by the aquiline coats of arms of the Norman kings. Elaborate designs border the pediment; on the bottom a meandering grapevine inhabited by birds, and along the slanting cornices a marvelous bestiary wanders; a sheep, a stag, a dragon, an owl, a hedgehog, a bat with a demon's face, and something approximating an elephant, as if the sculptor had never actually seen one.

Along with the main dome eighteen smaller domes were constructed in the seventeenth-century renovation. While these domes resulted in minor consequences for the exterior, inside the modifications were more dramatic. To support the heavy central dome a system of vaulting had to be designed, this replacing the now inadequate timber-frame roof. Whatever murals may have graced the medieval interior were destroyed.

Another addition to the interior was a heliometer or astrological calendar, where a small hole in one of the south aisle domes projects a point of sunlight on the floor. A line in bronze runs along the pavement, the signs of the zodiac arrayed along it: Capricorn, Aquarius, Leo, Pisces, and so on. At high noon on the summer and winter solstices it marks the changes of the seasons (the longest and shortest days of the year). The heliometer helped accurately mark special times of year, such as Easter, which is coordinated with the vernal equinox. Some might consider Palermo a backwater compared to Venice, Milan, or Florence, but when it came to things astrological Palermo held its own. The discoverer of the first asteroid in 1801 was Giuseppe Piazzi (1746-1826), a Palermitan mathematician and astronomer. He called it *Ceres* because that goddess was central to Sicily's mythology and was an embodiment of the island's historic importance as a grain producer. Our word 'cereal' is derived from her name. Piazzi was a monk from the Theatine Order and their home church in Palermo, San Guiseppe dei Teatini, is just a five-minute walk from the cathedral and is one of the best examples of Sicilian baroque in the city. Piazzi was honored by having a lunar crater named after him and when the thousandth asteroid was discovered in 1923 they called it 'One Thousand Piazzi'.

The royal Norman tombs rest in Palermo's cathedral. They cradle many of the corpses of the kings and queens of Sicily, including Frederick II, Holy Roman Emperor (r. 1220-1250), called by one fawning biographer *stupor mundi*, which doesn't mean he was in a stupor, but, rather, 'the wonder of the world'. The popes were far less impressed, especially at Frederick's religious skepticism. Pope Gregory IX excommunicated him and labeled him *Preambulus Antichristi* or 'Precursor of the Antichrist', though that's nothing compared to the accusations of a monk named Salimbene di Adam, who attributed to Frederick all manner of atrocities, from sealing people in barrels and watching to see if the soul would come out to raising children without exposure to language to see if they would develop a 'natural language' and, if so, which one? Hebrew? Greek? Evaluations of his character have to be taken with a grain of salt, however, since contemporaries also thought him strange because he bathed regularly.

Frederick, a German, attained his kingship of Sicily through his mother, Constance of Hauteville, the daughter of Roger II. He spent his thirty-year rule in Palermo where he carried on the enlightened traditions of the earlier Norman courts of Roger II and the Williams I and II. He had become king of Sicily at the age of three and was raised in Palermo, with Constance serving as co-regent until he came of age. Frederick was, in his time, probably the most powerful man on earth. Certainly he was one of the magnificent figures of the Middle Ages. His intellectual interests were broad and not just idle curiosity. He wrote the first known scientific book on birds, a treatise on falcons and falconry. It's still in print eight hundred years later. He founded the world's first state university in 1224, the University of Naples, and commissioned many scientific and literary works.

Sometimes you read that Dante was the first poet to use vernacular Italian instead of Latin, but Frederick's court supported a whole squad of poets who wrote in the vernacular before Dante, having adopted the chivalric themes of French verse imported by the Normans. In fact, it's possible that Dante got the idea of writing in Italian from the Palermitan poets. Pretty cheeky of Dante, then, to put Frederick in the Sixth Circle of Hell in his *Inferno*, amongst 'The Heretics Who are Burned in Tombs'. One of the poets of the Sicilian School, Giacomo dei Lantini, invented the sonnet, a form that dominated European poetry for centuries. I was thinking of these poems as I looked at Frederick's sarcophagus. No burning there. I guess Dante was wrong. Just a few feet away is the tomb of Frederick's first wife—he would have three—Constance of Aragon, who Frederick married in August of 1209 when she was twenty years old, but who died thirteen years later. Her crown is in the cathedral treasury, an extremely rare artifact of the Middle Ages. One of dei Lantini's most famous poems reads:

I have a place in my heart for God reserved,
So that I may go to Heaven,
To the Holy Place where, I have heard,
People are always happy and joyous and merry.

I wouldn't want to go there without my lady
The one with fair hair and pale complexion,
Because without her I could never be happy,
Being separated from my lady.

But I do not say that with blasphemous intent,
As if I wanted to sin with her:
If I did not see her shapely figure
And her beautiful face and tender look:
Since it would greatly comfort me
To see my woman shine in glory.

I preferred to have this in mind rather than Dante's harsh judgment. Romantic fantasies aside, Frederick is said to have had a mistress named Bianca Lancia, whom he married on her deathbed to legitimize their three children.

In 1781 Frederick's tomb was opened and legend has it he was in marvelous shape for someone six hundred years old. He still wore his regal clothing, decorated with precious stones. Wedged between Frederick's and Constance's tombs is the tomb of Henry VI (1165-1197), Frederick's father, behind which is the sarcophagus of Constance of Altavilla (1154-1198; daughter of Roger II and wife to Henry), and in the back left lies the founder of the line of Norman Sicilian kings, Roger II.

There's a story behind these tombs and the material most of them are made of, but one has to go back a bit to get the whole account. The story begins when King Roger was returning from a naval campaign when a storm struck his fleet. He prayed for deliverance and promised that wherever he landed he would build a cathedral in gratitude. Struggling through the tempest, his ships found refuge in the harbor of Cefalù, on the north coast of Sicily, and, good to his word, he built a magnificent church below the towering cliffs of the Rocca di Cefalù, an outcrop that, although smaller, rivals in impressiveness Palermo's Monte Pellegrino.

Roger had two porphyry sarcophagi made for the Cefalu cathedral, one for himself and the other for an heir or queen. He may have wanted Cefalù to become the official burial place for Norman royalty. The kings of France were buried in a specific church, St Denis in Paris, so it wasn't strange to designate an official repository for royal bodies. When Jean-Claude de Saint Non visited Palermo cathedral in 1778 he mused about the origins of the Palermo tombs: "The grandeur and beauty of these pieces of porphyry, have made it conjectured that these princes had despoiled some Roman heroes of their sepulchers… but why may not these princes… have brought back from the crusades, or procured by means of the fleets they sent hither, these blocks hewn in Asia?" Saint Non correctly observes that Roger's sarcophagi were made of porphyry, but they were not ancient tombs purloined from eastern lands. Few kinds of stone have a history as interesting as porphyry's. The stone's name is the Greek word for 'purple' and its main source was a quarry in Egypt, the *Mons Porphyritis* (the 'Purple Mountain'), which, according to Pliny, was found by a Roman soldier in the year 18 CE. It was a felicitous discovery, since the color purple was associated with emperors. The quarry was put under imperial monopoly.

The Roman emperors' use of porphyry was so extensive that they almost exhausted the Egyptian quarry, leaving the dregs for the later Byzantine emperors. In the imperial palace in Constantinople there was a special room, the *Porphyra,* with walls, floor, and ceiling paneled in porphyry slabs. The empresses would give birth to their children there. One of the names of an imperial Byzantine line made this concept literal: Porphyrogenitus ('Born into the Purple'). There are giant porphyry sarcophagi outside the entrance to the Istanbul Archaeological Museum, now empty and long ago shattered by thieves, quite possibly by Venetians who sacked Constantinople in 1204. Only members of the imperial family could use porphyry tombs, and thus the stone enveloped emperors when they came into the world and encased them when they departed it.[5]

In the twelfth century when Roger wanted porphyry he had to get it from Rome. Toppled porphyry columns that once graced ancient temples were quarried by medieval stone merchants from the city's classical ruins. During medieval times Christians thought nothing of pulling apart the ancient pagan temples built by the emperors who had persecuted them. Stone was stripped from these edifices to build the gleaming churches of the newly triumphant religion. It's likely that the tombs in Palermo were sculpted from sections of antique pillars. Sometimes the old columns were sawn into sections, like slices taken from giant salami, creating porphyry discs to be used in paneling or inlaid stone pavements, such as those at the Palatine Chapel or the Martorana, or, for that matter, the Sistine Chapel and many other early churches in Rome.[6]

Roger II was aware of the imperial associations of porphyry when he commissioned the two Cefalù sarcophagi, but when Roger died in 1154 his remains were brought to the Palermo cathedral and put in a different tomb; his body was never to rest in Cefalù and his dream of Cefalù as a resting place for Norman royalty was never realized. Poor Roger was never to inhabit the sarcophagus he had appointed for himself. Walter 'Ophamil',[7] the enigmatic and powerful archbishop of Palermo from 1169 to 1190, pulled rank on the clerics at Cefalù and demanded both of Roger's tombs. They lay in Palermo cathedral today, the one that Roger had made for himself cradling the remains of Frederick II and the other holding the body of Frederick's father, Henry VI, who unceremoniously evicted the body of the last Norman King, Tancred. Roger, rather unjustly, got the plain one tucked away in the back corner.

In the end Palermo cathedral didn't get all of the royal corpses, however, for in 1183 King William II, also known as 'William the Good' (r. 1166-1189) to distinguish him from his father 'William the Bad',

(Roger II's son)—who, as John Julius Norwich notes, more fairly should have been called 'William the Not So Bad'— had a rival cathedral and monastery built at Monreale not far from Palermo. It's so close that you can see the towers of Palermo cathedral, only 6.5 kilometers away as the crow flies. William II made tombs there for his father and himself, in porphyry and marble respectively, thus depriving Palermo of its monopoly on royal cadavers.

I took the winding staircase up the tower to the catwalk along the roof of the cathedral to the base of the dome. It was a beautiful morning with clear skies and a breeze that carried the invigorating snap of the highlands on its shoulders. The view northwards was great, and I could see Monte Pellegrino glowing in the distance with the bulk of the Teatro Massimo shrugging out of the city's lower structures. A modern high rise, the only one impeding an otherwise perfect view, made me wish I had a missile launcher. There was a young couple up there with a little boy who was tearing around and wanting to climb over the barriers. I appreciate kids like that. I have some friends whose son climbed over a bannister at the Los Angeles County Museum of Art and fell three stories onto a stone floor. Curators two decades later have nightmares of his mother's blood curdling scream resonating through the galleries as she watched her three year old plummet to the concrete. He only broke his arm. Great kid. No fear. As you can tell, I have no children of my own.

My next stop was the cathedral's underground crypt, filled with ancient Greek, Roman, and Early Christian tombs. On the way down I saw remnants of the old mosque that used to stand here before 1072. Parts of that structure, with distinctive Islamic designs, were integrated into the church. As I walked down the stairs into the subterranean damp I felt as if I was descending into history. In the Middle Ages wealthy people would appropriate classical tombs, kicking out the original—or at least the latest—inhabitants, reusing the sarcophagi (a word which, in ancient Greek, literally means 'flesh eaters'). Archbishop Walter is buried here, along with other Palermitan ecclesiasts. One worn but beautiful casket shows the hunting of the Calydonian boar from Greek mythology, probably dating from the fourth century BCE, and yet it cradles the remains of Archbishop Cesare Marullo, who died in 1588, two thousand years after the sarcophagus was made. It shows a team of hunters running about as they attack the legendary boar. The climactic moment is shown, with the heroine Atalanta reaching into her quiver for an arrow as Meleager deals the fatal blow with his spear.

Most impressive is a Roman tomb originally made for a poet. It's still magnificent even though someone, perhaps a dutiful Muslim, chipped off the faces of the figures, presuming they were depictions of pagan gods. The poet sits at the far right, being crowned with a laurel wreath by Calliope, the muse of epic poetry. The other eight muses accompany the poet and his wife, who is seated at the far left. One can make out Erato with her lyre, Euterpe with her flute, and Melpomene with her hand on a broken tragic mask. One of the muses offers the poet's wife something. Is it her husband's lyre, never to be strummed again to accompany his songs?

There's another notable Roman sarcophagus, this one showing a matrimonial scene, likely indicating it was meant to house husband and wife in death, reflecting their eternal devotion. At the center stands a priestess with the bride and groom standing in front of her. Birds are everywhere, symbols of good fortune. At the far left a woman plays a harp, supplying the wedding music. A Cardinal Tedeschi, who participated in the council of Basel and who died in 1445, the lid's inscription tells us, is the current occupant. It struck me as strange that a celibate Catholic churchman would have chosen a twelve-hundred-year-old pagan sarcophagus celebrating marriage to be entombed in.

After such a long time in the crypt with its funereal ambience I was happy to get into the sunlight and fresh air. I saw the same group of young Japanese tourists who'd been animatedly debating directions yesterday. They'd put away their maps and were clearly delighted at being somewhere they actually intended to be. The requisite portrait photos were being taken, with myriad groupings—this pair, that pair; this trio, that trio; this quartet, that quartet—and much chattering, with the cathedral as exotic backdrop. There were seven girls and only two boys; the boys reticent and receding, affecting cool, and the girls garrulous and giggly. I wondered if the guys were just along for the ride. The girls had a Hello Kitty innocence about them. One of the boys had a slick hairstyle. When it came time for his snapshot he flicked a black comb out of his back pocket, passed it over his head with studied seriousness, and smiled fetchingly while the girls twittered at his mock vanity. I ventured over and offered to take a picture of them together and they were so delighted that you'd have thought I'd offered world peace. Of course, this necessitated me posing with all of them; this pair, that pair; this trio, that trio.

Around the rectangular cathedral piazza, the dimensions of a soccer field, is a high fence populated by life-size statues of saints. They stand in stylish baroque contraposto, their draperies voluminous and undulating. Some watch tourists go by while others seem to beseech heaven to make them go away. If you look at their bases you can see their names inscribed, including the city's beloved female saints Rosalia, Ninfa, Christina, Oliva, Sylvia, and Agata. In most places the letters of the names are dots; little holes for the pins that once held metal letters in place. But this metal was gouged out long ago. In the 1890s there was a huge financial crisis in Italy and the lira was so worthless that the metal of coins was worth more as raw material than money, so many coins were simply exported and thus exchanged for more stable currencies. This led to inflated prices even for fairly common metals, including the bronze that the saints' names were written in. So for a while even bronze was worth stealing. Perhaps this explains the sorrowful look on some of these saints' faces; sad because so many Palermitani had to live in such desperate poverty. I imagine the perpetrators meekly begging forgiveness as they pried out the letters so as to feed their children for another day.

Afternoon

I'd had my fill of art and architecture for the morning and wanted a bit of relaxation, and when Palermitani want to relax they go to the seashore at Mondello. It's a wonderful half-hour bus ride that trundles below Monte Pellegrino through a park-like area on the western skirt of the mountain known as *La Favorita,* where there's a horse race track, the soccer stadium and other sports facilities. I glimpsed African women plying the sparse forests, looking exhausted after a night of turning tricks in this liminal strip of green at the edge of town. I saw the looming cliffs rock-climbers the world over come to ascend. These have endearing epithets such as "Never Sleeping Wall"; "Tears of Freedom"; "The Funeral Parlor" (*Pompa Funebre*; on this climb you get a view of a cemetery), and "The Slave" *(Lo Schiavo*). Go ahead and bring your ropes if you're interested. As for me, my idea of extreme sports was a walk on Mondello beach trying to find women in bikinis on a blustery May day, which, I gotta tell you, wasn't easy.

Much of the beach is public, though there are some private sections where people rent lounges and sun umbrellas. This commercialization of seaside real estate intensifies in the summer months. I've seen pictures in the high season where you can't see the sand for the people crammed on to it, but all the yellow parasols and blue plastic chaises were still folded up for the off season. I bought cannoli and cappuccino at a little beachside café and the barista made an elaborate flower design in the foam of my coffee.[8] It sounds corny but it cheered me up. It was such a pleasant place I indulged in a *granita* as well, the famed confection that was invented centuries ago in Palermo. In fact, they're sometimes called *granita Siciliana*. The Palermitan ones are so thick they're virtually like *gelato* and they come in dozens of flavors. Joseph Hager had some deserts like them in 1796 and described the varieties available even two hundred and eighteen years ago: "To temporize the heat which prevails in the morning… the inhabitants eat ices in the coffee-houses, where they have various kinds unknown to us; and if *sorbetti*, or the common ice, is not deemed sufficiently cold or refreshing, they have *gelati forti*, or a solid lump so completely frozen that it can only be divided by a knife… For this purpose snow is transported from the loftiest mountains in Sicily; from Madonia, the famous Eryx, and even from the summit of Etna... A number of small asses convey the snow, well packed in straw, where by the aid of salt any degree of frigidity can be given to it."

Mondello is a little suburban community gathered around the graceful crescent of Mondello Bay, which is monumentally superintended by the rocky headlands of both Monte Pellegrino and Monte Gallo. The waters were clear with a lovely hue and the sand was fine and white. There are several summer houses along the strand, built in the Art Nouveau / Liberty Style; even some designed by the great Ernesto Basile. But I was done looking at buildings for the day. The natural surroundings of Mondello were more compelling for the moment. Having said that, it was pretty hard to ignore the brassy Charleston restaurant and boardwalk, built in 1900 by the architect Rudolf Stualker, who drove pylons into the sea to erect this capricious eyesore. Its proper name is the *Antico Stabilimento Balneare di Mondello*, which just means the 'Old Mondello Beach Resort'. It sounds a lot classier in Italian. It imposes itself on the beach like an invading Art Nouveau UFO.

Mondello was founded ages ago around its *tonnara* or tuna cannery, now long gone since the low marshland around the bay was drained in the late nineteenth century and developed as a posh resort for Palermo's well-heeled gentry.[9] I took my shoes and socks off and waded in the cool water, making my way to the north part of the village where there's a tower and a little square surrounded by shops and restaurants. It was peaceful and it was hard to imagine the multitudes that would be here in two more months. I strolled along the wharf where small, colorfully painted fishing boats rocked softly on their moorings. One of them set out with two men in it, their little outboard motor spitting water and coughing blue smoke. Meanwhile, Monte Pellegrino changed its appearance moment by moment as churning cumulus clouds traversed the western sky. Colorless and dark one instant, rich tones would emerge once more as the sun irradiated its intricate stony faces, gray and rust, with groves of young pines cradled in the hollows. The wind was bracing and when the fishermen's diminutive craft cleared the shelter of the jetty it quavered in the chop, its mast swaying like a metronome. One of the men shoved the tiller, nosing the skiff into the whitecaps in pursuit of sardine or anchovy, while the other untangled the delicate blue filaments of their nets.

There was a nature trail nearby so I walked to the west and quickly found the entrance. An underachieving mafioso who lived in a camping van was exacting modest tribute from those who wanted to enter. Since he asked only fifty cents for pedestrians I barely broke stride to pay him off. The cliffs of Monte Gallo towered above me and all was silent. Bright tufts of grasses softened the serrated scree of rubble below the heights, punctuated with occasional bursts of lavender thistle. Around the pathway the fields were dusted with tiny blooms in yellow and purple; all under the stern observance of soaring limestone walls from which the shadowy maws of ancient caves invited exploration. The black silhouette of a hooded crow drifted slowly in an updraft along the silent walls. The path was a paved roadway, which grew narrower and narrower until it was just wide enough for a Fiat 500. After less than a kilometer I came upon an abandoned lighthouse. In one of the rooms someone had assembled a makeshift shrine to the '*Madonna del Faro*' or 'Madonna of the Lighthouse'. It didn't seem to be catching on. Of course, one good miracle could change all that. Just beyond Cape Gallo great boulders, thrown down long ago from the heights, were painted with the words *Zona Nudista,* which put a spring in my step as I reached for the 300 mm telephoto lens. Alas, there were no *nudistas* or even any non-*nudistas* to be found. The spot was certainly private enough, far from prying eyes. Here the cliffs were even more imposing, and to the west I could see the profile of the *Isola delle Femmine,* or 'Island of the Women', with its distinctive watchtower. It was getting on in the day and it was the end of the trail, so I headed back. Nearing Mondello again I saw an older man and woman on the seashore, stepping gingerly on slippery step-stones out to a small and uninviting point. At first I thought they carried fishing rods, but as I got closer I realized the cruelly gaffed poles were for hooking octopi out of their lairs.

I strolled around Mondello a bit more, but when I saw the bus I hopped on and went back to the city. The driver attempted to hit every pothole at maximum speed, as if he was trying to destroy the bus as quickly as possible. Perhaps he wanted a new one. When I made it back I sat on a curb in front of the Teatro Massimo, since the Piazza Verdi, like many piazzas in Palermo, is much in need of benches. Someone had left a newspaper so I picked it up and practiced my reading. There were a couple of sobering stories. Four *Caribinieri*, state policemen, had been arrested in Gela for involvement with a mafia organization. More disturbing was yet another story about refugees drowning in boats off the island of Lampedusa, which is a convenient stepping stone for Somalian, Libyan, Syrian, Sudanese and other African immigrants, just 138 kilometers at its closest point to the coast of Tunisia and 210 more to Sicily. More than 200 refugees had been saved, but 14 had died. In October of 2013, 111 boat people drowned and more than that number had gone missing, presumed dead. Their boat had sunk only a kilometer from the shores of Lampedusa. Many of the women and children couldn't swim and had no life preservers. Such were the risks people were willing to take to find a new life out of Africa and the Middle East's war-torn and impoverished states. In the past 15 years over 200,000 refugees have landed on the shores of Lampedusa, and the exodus continues unabated today.

I decided to go to Monreale tomorrow. I took out my map and figured that since Monreale was so close, and there was regular bus service, I'd have time in the morning to visit another monument that I was looking forward to seeing, a Norman pleasure palace with an Islamic name: La Zisa.

☙

DAY THREE

[Palermo] is traversed on every side by watercourses and springs; fruits grow in abundance; its buildings and walks are so beautiful that it is impossible for the pen to describe them or the mind to imagine them; everything is a real seduction to the eye.

-Abu Abdallah al-Idrisi, *The Book of Roger II*, c. 1154

Palermo…is in a district abounding in springs and brooks of water, a land of wheat and barley, likewise of gardens and plantations, and there is not the like thereof in the whole island of Sicily. Here is the domain and garden of the king, which is called Al Harbina, containing all sorts of fruit trees. And in it is a large fountain. The garden is encompassed by a wall. And a reservoir has been made there which is called Al Buheira, and in it are many sorts of fish. Ships overlaid with silver and gold are there, belonging to the king, who takes pleasure-trips in them with his women.

-Rabbi Benjamin of Tudela, *Travels*, 1170

Morning

At breakfast I met Patrice, a Canadian woman from Vancouver who's an amateur archaeologist. Every spring she volunteers to work on excavations. Sicily was her "favorite place in the world." No lounging on beaches for her. I'd gone down for breakfast at 7:00 and thought to make a quick job of it, but once Patrice got telling her stories we stretched it out to an hour, taking full advantage of both the buffet and each other's' company. Patrice was a real adventurer, even well into her sixties. She'd first visited Sicily in her twenties as a diver on an underwater excavation led by the marine archaeologist David Gibbins, who went on to have a successful career as a novelist, writing thrillers based on the exploits of his archaeologist protagonist, Jack Howard. I have to pay attention to these things just in case nobody buys this book. Patrice was leaving for a site near Salemi called Monte Polizzo, where teams have found artefacts dating back to the Bronze Age. We said our goodbyes, sincerely, as profound friendship can arise in a short time when one travels; it's a phenomenon I've long been fascinated by, and delighted by as well, many times over.

La Zisa was about two and a half kilometers from the hotel. As in the case of the Bridge of the Admiral, it's hard to believe that La Zisa was in the countryside at the outskirts of the city, beyond the walls and surrounded by forests and streams. Very close to the central Norman palace, King William II found it a convenient escape from the responsibilities of rule, able to sneak away to his retreat within ten minutes on horseback. A map produced in 1893 shows that even at that late date Palermo was still mostly confined by its city walls to the south and west, but had grown north along the spine of the Via della Libertà where the terrain was level and where the new port facilities were being developed. This expanded area came to be known as the *Nuova Città* or The New City where wealthy Palermitani built their villas. Now La Zisa is completely encircled by the modern metropolis except for the open space of the gardens, which have been recently fixed up with new fountains and fresh lawn. Don't walk on the grass. Not because you're not allowed to but because every dog owner in the vicinity thinks that the city of Palermo and the European Union taxpayers who supported the park's renovation put that new grass there solely for their dogs to crap in. And Palermitan dog owners do not pick up after their dogs. Why should they? They are a gift to you! They-are-SO-wonderful my little Fifi's poops! They are SO CUTE!!! Pretty Poo Poos! You should LOVE setting your camera bag down into them as you try to take a picture of La Zisa! Yes you should!

After a fusillade of vernacular English exclamations, all of them apparently well known to the two chuckling gardeners over there, I found a conveniently discarded popsicle stick. I was also well-supplied with alcohol wipes so the incident didn't detract too long from my enjoyment of La Zisa, framed by majestic pines and glowing a warm color in the morning sun. Along the top of La Zisa's façade a carved inscription in Arabic once ran, but today it is fragmented since blocks were taken away to make its roofline look crenellated like a fortress.

The letters are so eroded that they're almost illegible. I saw a section of several clay conduits all calcified together; water pipes for the medieval palace glued with lime deposits. It was pretty impressive. Parts of the old cistern, which also served as a pressure tower for the garden's fountains, also survive. I love that sort of thing. When I go to ancient Roman archaeological sites I pass the temples and go straight for the aqueducts and sewers. I'm a pragmatist.

There are some good artifacts in La Zisa, which is a museum today. Most impressive is a medieval brass bowl with silver inlay, about sixteen inches in diameter with a flaring edge. It's covered in Islamic script and scenes of courtly life, all done in intricate detail. La Zisa provided delights of all kinds; during the day gardens and hunting and at night wine and the embrace of lovers. In one of the upper rooms I was intrigued by a window that looked out towards the garden. There was a bench built into the wall beside it. I imagined young king William II reclining here, looking out over his domains. Today, regrettably, concrete high rises block one's view. In 1796, when Joseph Hager sat here, the panorama accorded with the original vista: "Here the observer enjoys a luxuriant prospect over the sea, the harbour, and the whole city; and, if he turns to the land side, he contemplates verdant fields and flowery meadows, and the tasteful villas surrounding Palermo."

The highlight of La Zisa is the large ground

-level room, partly open in the east through a large arch that faces the garden. This room, more like a portico, must have been filled with carpets, pillows and low tables, an oriental hall evoking the Alhambra in Granada or the palaces of the Ottoman sultans. Hager tried to imagine the scene: "...with cushions embroidered with gold... regaled with the sound of the oriental guitars, flutes, and cymbals, amidst the most fragrant perfumes, rose-water, and confectionaries." He also saw water running in the fountain: "At the entrance ... is an arched vault... lined with marble, in the midst of which a stream of fresh water discharges itself into a large marble basin, and is conveyed through the middle of the hall by means of a canal well contrived for the purpose." That fountain and water channels are still there. The most impressive of the surviving decorations are three mosaic roundels, the center one showing archers shooting birds in a tree and the flanking ones with peacocks eating dates from palms. They allude to the garden of La Zisa as a paradise on earth.

The rural palaces such as La Zisa were famous in medieval times and many visitors made note of them, including the Arab traveler Ibn Jubayr, who observed that "the king's palaces are disposed around the higher parts [of the city] like pearls encircling a woman's full throat. The king roams through the gardens and courts for amusement and pleasure. How many—may they not long be his—palaces, constructions, watchtowers, and belvederes he has!"

Ibn Jubayr often interjected provisos like "may they not long be his" or "may Allah destroy it" when he admiringly described something in Christian-ruled Sicily, bemoaning the fact that Sicily was no longer under the control of Islam.

The idyllic countryside of Palermo was not, however, solely a creation of the Norman kings. The twelfth-century historian Amatus of Montecassino records that when the Normans conquered the city in 1071, they found "... delightful gardens full of fruit and water... real things and earthly paradises." Appropriately, one of the palaces, with its attendant park, was called the *Genoardo,* an Italianization of the Arabic *Jannat al-ard,* which meant 'earthy paradise'. The name of La Zisa, too, had an Arabic derivation, from *al-aziz,* which means 'noble' or 'splendid'. La Zisa also figures in some Palermo's folk tales. The palace is thought to be inhabited by demons that protect an enormous treasure of gold, which will one day be discovered and make everyone in Palermo rich.

Another palace similar to La Zisa, called La Cuba, was not far away, but as I was walking there I noticed that I'd pass near the Capuchin catacombs. If gawking at thousands of dead bodies is your thing then Palermo's Capuchin catacombs are for you. The monks have been collecting corpses in underground tunnels for about three hundred years. By some estimates there are 8000 bodies there. A fan of zombie flicks would find all of this wonderful.

In 1885 Guy de Maupassant called them "frightful mummies, bearded and convulsed, which seem to howl, which seem afflicted by horrible pain." One expects eyes to pop open, as in the horror movies. Many of the bodies are hanging from walls, some lie in narrow niches, while others are in wooden boxes, but all are wearing their Sunday best in which they were entombed centuries ago. You can see women wearing the latest fashions from the 1700s or 1800s, though their crinolines are dried crisp and have already assumed the dun color of the dust their bodies will eventually become. Patches of hair still adhere to skulls, like the worst toupees ever. A nobleman's best suit hangs like a tattered rag about his skeleton. There's a wonderful shot in Luchino Visconti's film version of di Lampedusa's novel *The Leopard* (1963) where the Prince and his family attend a mass after a hot, arduous journey by horse cart. They're covered in dust, patiently enduring the service after their exhausting trip, reflecting their noble constitutions, but also visually anticipating the death of the social order to which they belong. Burt Lancaster, who plays the Prince of Salina, sits stuffed into his fine coat with his hair powdered by the dust of the road. One almost expects to see a desiccated Lancaster among these wizened corpses, his bony hand holding out a faded card with his filmography written out in elegant nineteenth-century cursive.

There are halls of them, a vast subterranean archive of death, for which a Capuchin librarian has worked out a morbid taxonomy. There's a corridor for children, their tiny bodies pathetic and shriveled, like dolls from an antique attic; a corridor for priests; a corridor for the Capuchin brothers themselves; a corridor for men; a corridor for women, but a special chapel for virgins; and even a corridor of *professionisti*: lawyers, doctors, apothecaries. As for the virgins, they looked just as bad in death as the non-virgins. Ladies, draw your own conclusions. De Maupassant singled out the women for a particularly vivid description: "Here are the women, yet more ludicrous than the men, for they have been decked out coquettishly. Their heads face towards you, clasped in lace- and ribbon-trimmed bonnets, a snow-like whiteness around these black, rotten faces, wasted by the strange workings of the earth. Their hands, similar to the cut roots of trees, emerge from the sleeves of new robes, and the stockings cover the bones of legs seem empty." The odd thing is there's no smell at all. The halls are so well ventilated that you'd think you were walking in a park.

Reverend Brian Hill went to Palermo in 1721 and explained how the bodies were cured, which I think he must have made up: "They are prepared for this situation by broiling them six or seven months upon a gridiron, over a slow fire, till all the fat and moisture are consumed." Patrick Brydone passed through fifty years later, in 1770, and he descended into these same caverns. He noted that Palermitan citizens visited ancestors often and even tried out their own niches for size. He says that some Capuchin monks slept overnight in the catacombs, thus having "visions." I think we'd call them nightmares. Generally, he was impressed by it all, writing, "I am not sure if this isn't a better method of disposing of the dead than ours. These visits must prove admirable lessons of humility… these dumb orators could give the most pathetic lectures upon pride and vanity." However, when William Henry Smyth visited in 1815 he was greatly offended by the place, saying "…it is difficult to express the disgust arising from seeing the human form so degradingly caricatured, in the ridiculous assemblage of distorted mummies, that are here hung by the neck in hundreds … so strangely altered by the operation of drying, as hardly to bear a resemblance to human beings."

There are dozens of signs in the hallways that say "No Photos" and emblems of cell phones and cameras with red lines through them. These are accompanied by signs that tell you that this is a sacred place and you should respect the dead by not taking pictures. But if the monks of the monastery really wanted the dead of their catacombs to be respected they wouldn't allow thousands of tourists to visit them every year to the tune of three Euros apiece for the price of admission. Their strategy is made evident at the exit and you're offered packets of postcards of those very corpses you weren't supposed to photograph. The Capuchins make substantial revenues from the exploitation of the corpse of a young girl, Rosalia, who died in the late 19th century at the age of five. The impressive quality of her mummification seems to have been driven by the recognition of the profits her prettiness could bring through time. She still draws money from the pockets of the faithful after more than a century.

The Capuchin monks were an early sixteenth-century offshoot of the Franciscans, founded by Brother Matteo da Bascio, who felt that the Franciscans of his time weren't living true to their founder's ideals of poverty. I'm not sure how turning a graveyard into a carnival show fits into that equation but I'm sure someone could explain it to me. Theology was never my strong suit. I guess viewing all those corpses is supposed to make you want to go out and accept Christ's salvation *subito*.

It's from the Capuchin monks that the name for cappuccino comes from. The word simply means 'little Capuchin'. I've heard a few explanations. One is that the brown coffee is the same color as the Capuchin monks' robes. More convincing is that the curling peak of whipped milk—showing that the froth is thick—resembles the monks' flopping hood. Either way, the monks missed out on copyrighting their order's name. They wouldn't have to sell tickets to their departed brothers' withering corpses. They also had a kind of monkey named after them. When these creatures were first seen in South America by European explorers they thought their color resembled the friars' habits.

From the catacombs it was a short walk to La Cuba, which was so well known in the Middle Ages that Boccaccio used it as a setting in one of his tales in the *Decameron*. Like La Zisa, it was a leisure palace of the Norman kings. Much later, in the seventeenth century, it served as the principal *lazaretto* or hospital during an outbreak of the plague. There are two Cubas, actually, one being very much like La Zisa in design, though smaller. As recently as 1810 it was used as soldiers' barracks, but not much more than its outer walls survives. Today, it's an empty shell with little to indicate its former grandeur. The Cuba Soprana is nearby, a tiny, open gazebo with a single dome, surrounded by orange trees in the garden of the Villa Napoli. These pleasure palaces were generously supplied with water from two principal rivers, the Kemonia and Papireto, which flowed through the medieval city. Maybe large streams would be more accurate descriptions of them. Along with the Oreto, their waters drove the mills of various industries. They filled the ponds and artificial lakes of the Norman kings' country villas and their waters circulated through fountains and bath houses. Like the ancient Romans, the Normans indulged in the luxury of water.

When Ibn Hawqal visited Palermo in 973 he wrote about the water supplies and wondered why the citizens took drinking water from stagnant wells when the streams provided such fresh water. His conclusion was that Sicilians ate too many onions:

"[they drink] ... water from wells ... rather than drinking the fresh running water due to their lack of healthiness and the abundance of onions in their diet, which ... is harmful to their senses." Hawqal claimed that the onions "damaged their brains, baffled their senses, affected their understanding, [and] diminished their comprehension." We have to take all this with a grain of salt because, truth be told, Ibn Hawqal didn't like Sicily very much. He saw the place as a backwater and thought Sicilians were the hillbillies of the Mediterranean. He was vexed because Christians had taken Sicily—the jewel of the Mediterranean—from the Muslims, but he was also appalled at the island's remaining Muslims. Of Palermo's Muslim religious teachers he ranted: "The teachers are ... in varying diverse stages of dementia and insanity in that they exceed the madness of teachers in any other country and of idiots in every other region." For Hawqal they were "dim-witted, deficient, [and] ignorant" and, tragically, "all the people of Sicily, in their simple-mindedness, believe that this group constitute their elite." Not a happy traveler, Ibn Hawqal.

Afternoon

I found myself on the Via Catalfimi where I waited for the bus to Monreale. There's an old photograph from around 1910 of a narrow-gauge electric rail going up there. People hang off the ends of the carriage like in the old cable cars in San Francisco. I wish they'd bring that back into service. Looks like fun. When the bus came it only took fifteen minutes to get to Monreale.

There are few edifices that embody the glory of the Middle Ages like the cathedral and monastery cloister at Monreale. They were founded in 1174 by the last Norman king of Sicily, William II. William must have been generous with funds, because the complex was able to house one hundred Benedictine monks merely two years after construction began. In 1185 Pope Lucius III raised Monreale to an archbishopric and in celebration the great bronze doors of the western portal were commissioned from the sculptor Bonanus of Pisa, with their dozens of Biblical scenes. William wasn't able to enjoy his remarkable church for long. He died on November 18th of 1189, at the age of thirty-four. He had become king under the regency of his mother, Margaret of Navarre, at the age of eleven, but in his short reign he accomplished much in terms of architectural patronage. The jewels of Monreale and La Zisa were his creations.

I entered the church from the elegant portico that runs along the building's north flank, through wonderful bronze doors with relief sculptures whose details have been erased by the acidic caresses of millions of faithful through history. The interior opens up its vast space, almost shocking in scale. It took me awhile to get my bearings. From the main west entrance to the apse, the distance of a football field, one's gaze is directed to the altar like a study in vanishing point perspective: all lines converging on the altar, the church's sacred focus. A mosaic of Christ Pantocrator watches over all, his eyes heavy lidded, almost sad, mourning the fate of mankind. His arms sweep out dramatically to embrace the whole curve of the semi-dome in which he resides. Below him the Virgin Mary holds court, enthroned and enveloped in her purple mantle called the *maphorion* and flanked by archangels and saints. On her lap a baby Christ in golden robes makes a blessing gesture and holds a scroll to show he's wise, like a Greek philosopher.

Immense monolithic columns, purloined from the ruins of ancient Roman temples, support rows of elegant arches along the flanks of the church. Above are registers of glimmering mosaics depicting scenes from Genesis, including the Creation of the World and the story of the Garden of Eden. Amazingly, not all tourists of the past were smitten by Monreale. John Galt, a curmudgeonly Brit who visited in 1809, described the architecture as being in a "mongrel style" and thought the mosaics were "not worth the trouble of putting on one's spectacles to look at." He must have been in a foul mood. I'll bet traveling in Sicily in the early nineteenth century was no picnic.

Noah makes appearances in the mosaics. Indeed, this expansive interior makes you feel like you're inside a massive ark, especially since the roofing retains its original construction with rows of painted timbers, almost like the inside of a ship's hull, though many beams had to be replaced after a fire in 1811, just two years after Galt's unsatisfactory visit. Noah directs a team of workmen to assemble his legendary vessel. They cut wood with saws and swing axes and adzes, a scene of industry echoing the carpenters' labors on the church eight centuries ago; an image given clearer articulation in the nearby scene of the building of the Tower of Babel, where masons hew stones, mix mortar and build walls. Elsewhere Noah gathers animals aboard the ark, though his ship seems no larger than a rowboat. In another tableau bodies float in the floodwaters as a crow pecks at a corpse, grim reminder of God's wrath even as the dove bears the olive branch to Noah's outstretched hands. Post flood we see Noah making wine by crushing grapes from a vine, as if he's wringing out a sponge. Next to it the sad effect: Noah's sons dealing with their drunken father. An entire moral universe thus unfolds.

In the south transept are the tombs of both king Williams, a porphyry one for William I and a marble one for his son. From near the tombs I got a good look at the Pantocrator and a mosaic of Christ crowning William II. In the latter, William bows his head, his hands in a worshipping gesture. He wears a bejeweled robe of Byzantine splendor as Christ places the crown on his head and angels deliver the implements of authority, the scepter and the orb. He holds an open Bible to the "I am the light of the world" text that's also in the Pantocrator image. An inscription floats around William's head: *MANUS ENIM MEA AUXILIABITUR EI*, from Psalm 88:22 of the Vulgate Bible, "My hand shall help him (and my arm shall strengthen him)", a verse that refers to King David, indicating that William's reign, too, is blessed by God. Right below this mosaic is the king's elevated throne platform. I imagined him sitting there—that young king well known and even adored for his good looks—in regal splendor, the divine source of his authority unambiguously articulated by the image above him.

There's no fee to get into the church, so I didn't balk at paying for the extras, which included access to the north transept of the church. From there I saw the pendant to the coronation mosaic, the dedication mosaic, which shows William on bended knee approaching the enthroned Virgin. She accepts the architectural gift of the church—it looks like a particularly sumptuous Lego model—while from heaven God's hand extends a blessing towards William. These images eloquently articulate the relationship between divine and secular power. William builds the church and, in exchange, Christ confers power to William and his lineage. It's a perfect example of how religion and politics, sacred and secular, were inexorably intertwined in the medieval order of things.

Another extra, also well worth it, is going up one of the towers to a catwalk along the south roofline of the church, providing a great view of the monks' cloister and a stupendous vista towards Palermo. I could see for miles in the clear spring air and the Conca d'Oro, which the sixteenth-century Sicilian historian Tommaso Fazello called "an amphitheater imagined by nature," was a picturesque green perimeter after the spring rains. John Dryden visited Monreale in the year 1700 and rhapsodized about this same view: "When we came up to near Monreale, we looked down on the left side of us and beheld one of the most pleasant and richest valleys in the world, and which looked green... being full of olive trees, orange and lemon trees... The prospect is so pleasant and so far exceeding the prospect of any valley I ever saw in my life, that it would be a rash attempt to describe it."

After descending the tower's winding staircase I went to buy my ticket for the cloister. The woman at the wicket tried her best to give me the pensioner's reduced price, which I appreciated at the financial level but not so much on the ego level, since I'm not even close to sixty-five. Nevertheless, she finally asked me for the full six Euros, and looked at me apologetically, as if she was ashamed to charge such a pathetic looking old codger the full price of admission. Later, I looked at myself in a restroom mirror. I was unshaven, more than a bit mussed, and looked decidedly haggard. I could see her point. I made a mental note to shave and get a haircut.

Travelers through many ages recorded their impressions of the cloister and its sculpted capitals. The French nobleman Nompar II de Caumont visited in 1420 and observed, "all around this cloister there are alternating pairs of columns, of lovely workmanship: finely wrought and with interlaced capitals; and others entirely covered in mosaics of gilded stones." Monreale's cloister has over a hundred intricately sculpted capitals, blooming like ornate lilies atop their slender columns, opening to the radiance of the Sicilian sun. I imagined a winter day centuries ago, gray with light rain falling, wisps of mountain mist drifting through the arcades on chill air, monks with bowed heads, nodding as they slowly walked under the sheltering vaults—as much to keep warm as aid contemplation—counting on their rosaries the prayers for living and dead. The sculptures might direct the brothers towards virtue, distract them with capriciousness, or even tempt or entertain them. St Bernard of Clairvaux (1090-1153), a member of the ascetic Cistercian Order of monks, expressed his opinions about such images in a text called the *Apologia*: "What excuse can there be for these ridiculous monstrosities in the cloisters where the monks do their reading, extraordinary things at once beautiful and ugly? Here we find filthy monkeys and fierce lions, fearful centaurs, harpies, soldiers at war ... Over there is a beast with a serpent for its tail, a fish with an animal's head... One could spend the whole day gazing fascinated ... instead of meditating on the law of God. Good Lord, even if the foolishness of it all occasions no shame, at least one might balk at the expense."

In Monreale's cloisters one can find all the subjects Bernard abhorred, and more, though there are also many that portray religious stories, as if the two kinds of subject matter reflected a battle between the sacred and profane. The subtext of Bernard's criticism was a critique of the Cluniac order of monks, which had grown wealthy and influential in France and whose monasteries were richly decorated with sculptures. The Cluniacs wore black robes, the Cistercians white, and thus they were known as Black Monks and White Monks respectively. For Bernard, their respective monastic ideologies were also black and white. Against the Cluniacs Bernard preached austerity, a return to simple monastic life. Yet Bernard was far from simple himself, and while he feigned courageousness he was in many ways a coward. When challenged by the great intellectual Abelard to theological debate, Bernard had Abelard condemned. His sermons were so inflammatory that surges in Christian fanaticism led to massacres of Jews in Germany. He was the prime promoter of the disastrous Second Crusade, which cost tens of thousands of lives. Everywhere one looks in Bernard's biography one finds him guilty of a singular and definitive sin: Vanity, the very sin he so often saw in others. The Machiavellian Bernard could deftly change his opinions if it profited him. For years he excoriated Roger II of Sicily—he'd called him "*tyrannus Siciliae*", "tyrant of Sicily"— but later became obsequious to the ruler, writing fawning and deferential tracts while earlier he'd hurled all manner of invective. It is hard to think of any monk who was so political and influential. It would be three centuries before the Christian West saw a monk whose radical activities equaled, or even surpassed, Bernard's. His name was Martin Luther.

Monks are supposed to renounce the pleasures of the world, yet their monasteries are found in the most beautiful locations. The vista from Monreale must have been even more glorious in the past. The Conca d'Oro, with its gentle and verdant talus fanning out below the Royal Mountain, was luxuriant with groves like the ones Dryden saw. In the distance was, and still is, the brilliance of Palermo with its many domes against the cerulean sea beyond. Through this fertile crescent the waters of several mountains irrigated groves with centuries-old trees. In 1840 A. J. Strutt noted that "the neighbourhood abounds with magnificent olive trees, which date their origins from the time of the Saracens and hence many of them are arrived at a size rarely witnessed. One, in particular, measured twenty-two paces around at the roots, and has a head flourishing in proportion."

The Conca d'Oro wasn't always so serene and fresh. There was a time in the fifteenth-century when speculators used the area for sugar production, which reached industrial proportions. The energy demands of the process turned the Conca d'Oro into a miserable place. Water had to be boiled in huge cauldrons, necessitating the burning of wood, which led to the deforestation of the surrounding mountains. The pollution was so bad that in 1417 the city had to regulate the industry's traffic. Sugar cane depleted the soil and consumed enormous amounts of water, requiring the construction of the Ficarazzi aqueduct in 1443. Accounts from 1472-73 indicate that 152 tons of wood were burned to produce 3143 loaves of sugar. Potters did well when sugar was king, as the molds were destroyed in the process, thus necessitating a steady supply of new ones. As I looked over the lucid expanse below me I imagined being a monk here in the late fifteenth century and cursing the clouds of smoke spoiling my formerly pristine mountain refuge.

The dormitory of the original monastery, which had its long south side facing this lush panorama, was early beset with architectural instability. As early as 1382—though by then the buildings were two centuries old—papal documents note the structural problems at Monreale. In 1420 Nompar II de Caumont sadly noted that the buildings were "...put up so long ago that it is all crumbling; it is a great loss to let such a work collapse in this manner." A description by Antonio di Lello, from 1596, observed that in that south side "only the walls are standing." Photographs from around 1900 show the broken arches looking like a huge barn with its roof blown off. By then, the monk's quarters and refectory had been moved to more stable ground to the west.

I lost track of time whilst studying the capitals, finding it true what Guy de Maupassant wrote in 1885, that "the marvelous cloister of Monreale … transmits to the soul such a feeling of gracefulness that one would like to remain there almost indefinitely." The capitals he described as "sculptures of incomparable fineness." On one of them parents watch as their children leap like acrobats. On another knights joust, while elsewhere soldiers do battle with broad swords, sometimes with each other and sometimes with lions or tigers. Strange beasts, of the kind Bernard decried, populate several scenes: centaurs and mermaids, sirens and dragons, griffons and serpents. In one King William II offers the church of Monreale to the Virgin Mary who has the infant Christ on her lap. Mary opens her hand as if to say, "Look at this great church he's offering you!" An inscription reads *REX QUI CUNCTA REGIS SICULI DATA SUSCIPE REGI*, a caption for the event: 'The King of Sicily gives [the church] to the King of All [Christ]'.

Another sculpture shows the Roman Emperor Constantine and his mother Helena holding the cross, commemorating Helena's discovery of the True Cross in the Holy Land in the early fourth century. Constantine has a beard and Helena looks very serious. Her breasts are mere nubs and on her neck, holding her vestments together, is a Celtic brooch—similar to the famous Tara brooch, one of the world's most extraordinary pieces of jewelry—perhaps an indication of the French origins of the sculptors who would have known Celtic culture.

In the Garden of Eden Adam and Eve reach into the tree of knowledge for the forbidden fruit. In the next scene the angel expels the penitent couple from paradise through a sturdy looking door, while in the following act Eve sits on a rock and mopes in her coarse wool dress as Adam hoes a field and says "Look what I have to do now!" One of my favorite capitals shows men holding huge birds with human heads. Bernard wouldn't have liked it.

The Nativity is a packed scene. On the upper left is a beaming star with a swaddled Christ child below. Mary, having just gone through labor, is offered some fruit for nourishment. To the right angels call the shepherds, who tend sheep with their faithful dog on a rocky hilltop. They've hung their lunch sacks in the branches of a tree. One of the most dramatic scenes is the Massacre of the Innocents, with Herod ordering the killing of the male babies of Judea. Soldiers wrest squirming infants from their mothers' arms and raise their swords to strike. In the end the mothers wail beside a pile of dead babies, a Roman column in the background to indicate the guilty. The variety of styles makes you wonder how many sculptors' workshops were working here. Only one capital has an autograph inscription, reading *EGO ROMANUS FILIUS COSTANTINUS MARMURARIUS* ("I am Romanus, the son of Costantinus, sculptor in marble").

The quartets of columns in the corners are themselves carved in swirling vines and figures. Several others have geometric patterns in mosaic, which have many pieces missing. In 1840 when A. J. Strutt had lunch with the monks he noted that, "... the adjoining cloister... [is] adorned with upwards of two hundred columns, each of different device, and inlaid with mosaic... [they] excited my utmost admiration. The mosaic, however, has suffered from the idle industry of the soldiers quartered in the convent, in the time of the troubles, for they amused themselves by picking out a great part of it."

When I left the cloister I felt as if I was leaving a remarkable alternate world behind, and as the sun descended in the west I saw the bus in the piazza so climbed aboard and went back to Palermo. I was getting hungry and decided to look around in some of the nicer places for a good meal where I could write in my notebook and try some hearty Sicilian dishes like Pasta alle Sarde. Usually, I eschew fancier restaurants, especially when traveling. Firstly, there's the cost. Secondly, I find the simple food that ordinary people eat is usually the best. Recipes are democratic. I came upon a slick looking place in the old city. It had a nice ambience, though the starched white table clothes raised an alarm in my wallet; so, too, the tiny Christmas lights strewn in the potted ficus trees in the otherwise shadowy outdoor section and the lectern at the entrance, where there was a book with reservations in it. The place was empty so I thought I could risk refusal. I stood by the lectern and waited patiently, studying menu items that read like Italian haikus. Finally, a young man came out. He smiled brightly and called out cheerily, "*Buona Sera*", followed by a brief pause and "Are you dining alone, sir?" To which I sheepishly replied, "*Si*".

There are forty-three different muscles in the human face, making it an incomparably sophisticated register of emotion. When the young man had come out all of those muscles were taut, activated by the promise of a profitable commercial transaction. He was doubtless thinking I was the early-bird of a large group of rich tourists, but when he found that I was alone every one of those muscles dropped into a pool of slackness, but only after having gone through a microsecond in which his face registered a grotesque rictus of the kind you'd find in a horror movie involving corpses rising from the dead. I momentarily had an unappetizing flashback to the Capuchin catacombs. He rallied poorly and gestured for me to follow him into the restaurant. He paused briefly when we entered, scanning the expanse before him, full of empty tables but for one along the far wall where a group of four was mid-meal. "*Piacere,*" he said, flatly. We headed for a dark corner. For a moment I thought he was taking me to the men's room, having misunderstood my reason for visiting. It took a moment for my eyes to adjust to the gloom but, indeed, there was a table for two lurking in the shadows like a mafia hit man. I sat down and nodded my thanks. He replied by gathering up with a censorious clatter the second plate, placemat, glasses and set of cutlery. What about the lonely, beautiful Swedish woman who is sure to arrive in a few minutes and want an art historian for company? He cleared the table with such petulance that I bet if he'd had scissors he'd have cut the table cloth in half and whipped it away with a flourish. Two scrawny flowers hung their heads in a tiny vase. I half expected him to pluck one of them out. He handed me a menu, on the run, as if he had more important things to take care of in his empty restaurant. I looked at the menu for some time and finally decided on the simplest and next-to-least-expensive thing. I waited. The waiter had gone somewhere in the occult regions of the kitchen, or perhaps was having a smoke in the alley. Or two smokes. Or half a pack. Anyway, I opened the menu again and realized that when I ordered he'd give me a contemptuous look and I'd have to deal once more with what was already an unpalatable attitude. I realized that I'd lost my enthusiasm so placed the menu on the table and walked out. Perhaps the waiter had been at a small altar in the back, praying to St Martha that I'd leave (she's the patron of waiters and waitresses because she always fed Jesus and his apostles). In a few minutes I came across a *panificio* and a friendly proprietor made me a fresh sandwich of mortadella sprinkled with lemon juice. Even after a long day of serving people he cheerily welcomed me and my modest business with a wide smile and a "*Grazie*" and "*Buona sera signor! Buon appetito!*" I took the panini and a cold bottle of Orangina to a small park and sat on a bench and watched grandmothers do embroidery while their grandchildren roared around on tricycles. I was glad I had the good sense to walk out of that restaurant, leave that waiter with his surliness, and instead dine joyfully on my bench with the vibrant life of this wonderful city unfolding before me.

DAY FOUR

We are now arrived at [Palermo] the great capital of Sicily; which is in our opinion in beauty and elegance is greatly superior to Naples. It is not, indeed, so large, but the regularity, the uniformity, the neatness of its streets and buildings, render it more pleasing; it is filled with people who have mostly an air of affluence and gaiety.

-Patrick Brydone, June 23, 1770

Morning

After four nights at the Excelsior I was getting worried about the escalating bill. The Excelsior had originally been built in 1891 as part of the *Esposizione Nazionale* held in Palermo that year, where artisans and manufacturers from all over Italy displayed their wares in grand pavilions. Most of the structures were temporary, but the Excelsior became one of Palermo's grand hotels. I appreciated its *fin de siècle* grandeur but from the start I'd planned to stay only a few nights to get rid of my jet lag. My dwindling finances obliged me to go to the front desk and check out. I was hoping they'd say "We hear you are writing a travel book on Palermo and we'd like you to stay here for free as long as you like for the service you're doing our great city!" Alas, the receptionist just swiped my card with silent efficiency.

I found a much cheaper place in the old town. The Excelsior, for all its comforts, wasn't that close to the historical center, and I wanted to walk out of my door and go right to exploring the city's most interesting quarters. My luggage in tow, I hopped on the 101 bus that goes along the Via della Libertà, lined with lovely Plane trees (*Platanaceae;* Americans call them Sycamores). I got out at the Teatro Massimo in the Piazza Verdi.

The little pension called Casa Sicilia was just behind the theater on the Via Volturno, a street that makes up for its short length with plenty of charm and a row of ficus trees shading a wide sidewalk where immigrants sell stuff from tables they set up every day. One had 1960s Italian bodice-ripper novels with great titles and lurid covers with couples in passionate embraces: *La Vergogna di Purity* ('The Shame of Chastity') and *Come Vele al Vento* ('Like a Sail in the Wind'). I thought about buying one so I could bolster my vernacular Italian but thought better of it when I envisioned myself handcuffed to a stranger's bed owing to a careless misapplication of a pronoun.

The Casa Sicilia was the kind of funky place I used to stay in when I was a backpacker in my twenties. I could have had a bed in a dormitory room with other travelers but I was feeling too old for that. No rooms had their own bathroom; twenty people shared one for men and one for women. The bed in my room was so small it gave new meaning to the term 'single bed'. It was so narrow that you couldn't roll over from your right side to your left without shifting back to the side you were shifting from. There were springs that stuck out right in the middle of what one could only very loosely call a mattress, so you had to negotiate those as well, making sure no projecting bones met up with them. They were army cots, basically, or perhaps cots the Italian army had rejected but were deemed fit for foreigners who could no longer afford the plush cradles of the Excelsior. The pillow had the consistency of a slab of liver, as happens with foam rubber over the course of ten-thousand heads. I dared not take off the threadbare polyester pillowcase. There are some things one just doesn't want to know.

I shouldn't complain. Travelers in ages past had worse experiences. In 1796 when Joseph Hager travelled through Sicily he noted that "there are no inns, but those that are so miserably inconvenient that the traveler finds himself necessitated to lodge in a monastery." The Casa Sicilia wasn't quite that austere. There was a tiny balcony and a place to hang laundry. The rooms didn't have numbers but names. My room was called 'Tropical', referring to the African decoration and vivid orange walls. In the summer I bet it was tropical, but that's why I was here in early May. Other room designations included 'Blue Sky' and 'Freedom', which gives you an idea of the general grooviness. While for the twenty-something backpacker it doesn't get much better than this, for the over-fifty with the Briggs and Riley roller it's a bit scary. Essentially it's a youth hostel, but if you're my age and just can't afford better, then, well, best just relive the past and be glad you're not back on that park bench in the Villa Giulia gardens.

Older guests, I reckoned, were rare. The proprietress, a wonderful woman named Giulia, looked at me askance when I came in, but less askance when I said I wanted a room for three weeks. Her eyes shifted from leery to the Euro sign. At the time I was her only guest, though others trickled in in the coming days. She was happy for the walk-in windfall. Nowadays, young budget travelers make reservations on their smartphones. I'm always a few years behind the times.

There was a common kitchen at the Casa Sicilia and a small breakfast area. The free Wi-Fi worked like a charm and the place was very clean thanks to an amiable guy from Ghana named Reggie who liked Reggae and played it loudly while he swept floors to the beat. There was an eclectic collection of African musical instruments, mostly drums, hanging on the wall, along with paintings done by someone who, shall we say, was not a professional painter, or a semi-professional painter, or, truth be told, an amateur painter. Nevertheless, it all lent color to the place and, what the hell, I can't paint either. Testimonials from giddy twenty-year-old backpackers from Poland were posted: "I [Heart] Casa Sicilia! -Gdansk!" with similar sentiments echoed in Swedish, Czech, and other languages I didn't recognize. Tips for local travel, bus and train schedules, pamphlets for hostels all over Europe, and other helpful hints were tacked up everywhere, as were reminders about turning off lights, cleaning dishes, disposing of refuse and, over the communal stove, "Close well the gas is dangerous! Like a bomb!" should any Americans only familiar with electric stovetops be careless with the knobs and their cigarettes. At night, with every light in my room on, I still had to use a flashlight to read because, as several signs posted throughout reminded patrons, "We are not a Power Plant"! Indeed not. Nor do I have the eyes of an owl. The building had a history, too. It was one of three late nineteenth-century blocks built in a row just behind the Teatro Massimo, and I was told that they were designed by the great Palermitan architect Ernesto Basile.

The people who worked at the Casa Sicilia were wonderful and we often ate take-out meals together from the Trattoria del Monsu across the street, which made traditional Sicilian dishes to order, such as involtini, Pasta alla Norma (with eggplant), and Pasta alle Sarde (with sardines). It was a fantastic experience. It sure wasn't like the encounter Patrick Brydone had when he stayed in Palermo in 1770: "We are but indifferently lodged; however, it is the only inn we have seen in Sicily, and indeed may be said to be the only one in the island. It is kept by a noisy, troublesome French woman who I find will plague us; there is no keeping her out of our rooms, and she never comes in without telling us of such-a-prince and such-a-duke, that were so superlatively happy at being lodged in her house: we can easily learn that they were all desperately in love with her; and indeed she seems to take it very much amiss that we are not inclined to be of the same sentiments …I believe we must take more notice of her, otherwise we shall most certainly have our rent raised; but she is as fat as a pig and as ugly as the devil."

A few years later, Reverend Brian Hill stayed in the same guesthouse, but the woman Brydone wrote of had passed away, though her husband still ran the inn. Hill wasn't very happy with the accommodations either and thought them too expensive for what he got: "…we pay full three guineas a week, and near five shillings a-piece for our miserable repast at dinner, servants apart." It's hard to feel sorry for anyone who could afford servants.

As for location, the Casa Sicilia is fantastic. The Via Volturno leads to the Porta Carini, the entrance to one of Palermo's best open markets, the Mercato del Capo. And in less than fifteen minutes along that picturesque and boisterous alley you come out at a little piazza that, while totally neglected, affords a magnificent view of the apses of the cathedral in the morning sun, with their wonderful black volcanic stone inlays in different geometric designs. There I saw a sign, "Sicilian Cart Museum," pointing to a narrow lane, and there, indeed, was one of Palermo's treasures. I'm not sure if 'museum' was quite the word. Part of it seemed to be open air, with carts parked in the alley. The proprietor didn't have enough space for all his artefacts, which is unfortunate because some of the carts were deteriorating, exposed to the elements.

The old Sicilian peasant carts (*Carretto Siciliano*) were once the most ubiquitous public art form of the island. Alas, these rustic conveyances are part of Sicily's disappearing traditional culture. For centuries ordinary families took great pride in them. When John Stoddard visited Palermo in 1905 he was completely charmed and called them "the most extraordinary carts I had ever seen". He wrote that, "not only are the axels, wheels, and shafts elaborately carved; they are adorned with rings and stripes of red and green, while on the four sides of the cart are painted with portraits, allegorical figures, or representations of historical incidents…which… astonish the beholder by the number, variety, and character." Since the wealthy of Palermo had fine carriages, the working people wanted to show them up by making their humble work carts more attention-getting. Their horses and donkeys, too, were bedecked with colourful trappings. The stories painted on the side panels ranged from the historical to the mythological, but the preferred tales were the same ones loved in the Sicilian puppet theater, another important vernacular art form, especially in Palermo.

In fact, there's a puppet museum in the city as well, named after the famous scholar of Sicilian puppetry, Antonio Pasqualino. In the Middle Ages the Normans brought their poetry and songs to Sicily, especially those involving Charlemagne and his hand-picked entourage of knights, the legendary Paladins. Norman rule in Sicily was relatively brief, but the stories of the Paladins remained in the popular culture and flourished, particularly in Palermo where even today one can see marionette performances. They give regular shows at the museum where you can see them in action, cracking each other over the head with their swords. The most popular tales involve the knights Roland and Renaud, who are both complements and foils to one another. They're cousins, and their characters are often altered in Palermitan puppet shows, sometimes reflecting mafiosi or *banditti*. One could argue that the puppet shows were Palermo's most characteristic historical art form, so deeply did they permeate the culture of the city in the days before film, radio, television, and the internet drove both the puppets and carts into museums, making artifacts of what were once truly living art forms. I was musing about these stories as I studied a panel with a cartoon-like Paladin running through a Turk, blood spurting everywhere. I was also wondering what to do next. I looked at my watch and realized, since it was a bit later in the day, the Palatine Chapel was less likely to be crowded. It was only five minutes away. I made a dash for it.

The Palatine Chapel is ensconced in the fabric of the medieval Norman palace and is entered through a graceful renaissance courtyard called the Cortile Maqueda, a later addition dating from the time of the Spanish Viceroys. On a wall outside the chapel is a trilingual inscription in Latin, Greek, and Arabic, which commemorates the construction of a sophisticated clock in March of 1142. The clock, in the Middle Ages a high-tech device, was likely designed by the Muslim scholar Muhammad Al-Idrissi, the most famous intellectual of Roger's entourage. Al-Idrissi was also a geographer and in 1154 he produced the *Tabula Rogeriana* (The Book of Roger), which included the most remarkable map created in the medieval period. It purports to show the world, but then much of the world was unknown, so it only shows sketchy versions of Europe, North Africa, the Middle East, and Asia. North is at the bottom, so it looks upside down to us. The book's title in Arabic was "A Diversion for Men Longing to Travel to Faraway Lands", which sounds a lot more interesting than "The Book of Roger." The most accomplished intellectual of Roger's court, Al-Idrissi's works are still admired today.

The Normans were Catholics, but they conquered an island that had once been Byzantine Greek, and therefore Orthodox, but which had been ruled by Muslim Arabs for almost three centuries.

The chapel's decoration reflects artistic traditions from all three cultural traditions. Guy de Maupassant visited the Palatine chapel in 1885 and christened it "the most beautiful in the world, the most surprising religious jewel dreamed up by human thought." When Edward Hutton visited around 1925 he echoed the sentiments of many earlier visitors through history, noting that it was "one of the loveliest and most fascinating works of art left in the world." Every wall is draped with sumptuous mosaics. The chapel is by no means small; it was for court ceremonies, not intimate devotions. The ceiling is made of painted wood, much of it constructed in complex multifaceted designs made by Arab craftsmen who remained after the Norman conquest of the island. Around them are inscriptions of auspicious words in Arabic, such as 'Health', 'Prosperity', 'Blessing', and 'Perfection'. In some of the panels are images of rulers, perhaps representing Roger II himself, seated cross-legged like a Muslim potentate.

Even the flooring is opulent, with geometric designs of inlaid marbles such as serpentine breccia, porphyry, and *cipollino* marble. Philagathos, the homilist of King Roger II's court, delivered a sermon in which he compared the colorful pavements to a meadow of flowers, but noting that, while spring blooms fade, the richness of the flooring would retain its vivacity for centuries, "preserving in itself an eternal spring." Another contemporaneous twelfth-century chronicler, Romuald of Salerno, wrote that: "King Roger...ordered a very beautiful palace to be built at Palermo, in which he constructed a chapel floored in astonishing stone, which he covered with a gilded roof, and adorned and beautified with various ornaments." These praises could have been written today, so beautifully preserved is this medieval wonder.

When you go in it's as if you've entered a golden cavern filled with spectacular iridescent imagery. The walls and ceiling oscillate with energy and instability. Figures float in a vacant ether; Noah's mosaic ark is buoyed on wiggling lines; God creates the animals of the world, which advance out of nothingness, animated by color and light, two by two in serried ranks. He breathes life into Adam with a magical ray emanating from his mouth; the tower of Babel is built by industrious masons; St Peter is freed from prison by an angel while the guards lie unconscious below; the blind, Old Testament patriarch Isaac feels the hands of his son Jacob, covered in fur mittens, thinking they are the hirsute hands of his twin brother, Esau, who is thus deprived of his patrimony through deception.

Towards the altar, on the sides of the central arch, are the archangel Gabriel and the Virgin Mary. She raises her hand, startled by the abrupt appearance of the celestial being. From the crest of the arch God's hand reaches out of a cloud, sending the dove of the Holy Spirit towards Mary on a beam of light. In many Annunciation scenes Mary is shown reading the Old Testament prophecy regarding this very moment: "And the Lord himself shall give you a sign. Behold, a virgin shall conceive, and bear a son, and shall call his name Immanuel" (Isaiah 7:14). But here she is shown spinning. The symbolism is that the pure spirit of God is interlacing itself into the flesh of the Virgin's body. The oval spindle of white thread is a metaphor for Mary's pure womb, but a gold thread has appeared in it, indicating that a king's body is now entwining with her untainted flesh.

Another wrinkle in the Annunciation story is that Mary was thought to have become impregnated through her ear, that is, by simply hearing the announcement of the archangel, thus retaining her virginity. This may be why in Annunciation scenes Mary tilts her head a bit, as if she's listening. Hearing the Word of God, she obediently accepts it, literally, incarnated into her body.[10]

I struck up a conversation with a couple from New York, Roger and Jan Gordon, who decided to come to Sicily when friends allayed their fears about the mafia. The association between crime and Sicily has made tourists reticent. I call it The Godfather Effect. In a café in Santa Barbara I once saw a woman looking at travel brochures for Italy, so I said hello. I mentioned Sicily and she made a grimace: "SICILY! Well, I'd never go there!", then drew a finger menacingly across her throat. Rural Tuscany was her Italian dream, that 'Under the Tuscan Sun' fantasy.

You know, where being kidnapped by a local man is something you'd want to happen. I defended Sicily and told her of the people I'd known who had gone there without incident. "As safe as Tuscany!" I assured her, but she looked at me sidelong, as if I was a Clandestine Agent of the Sicilian Tourist Board. She gathered up her pamphlets and high-tailed it to the reassuring mass of her SUV, leaving me quite dejected.

Roger in particular liked being on an island which, in its most illustrious age, had a king also named Roger. Jan had already begun calling him Roger III when he got too bossy. They'd arrived two days before and were going to rent a car and tour the island for two weeks. Sicily is shaped like a triangle—a fact that also gave the island one of its ancient names, *Trinacria* ('Three Cornered')—only about 280 kilometers (175 miles) wide at its widest. It has a good highway system, so you can drive from one end to the other in less than four hours. We talked about the advantages of being here in the spring, and I told them they'd see a countryside as green as Ireland, with wildflowers blooming everywhere. There are thousands of towering new windmills in the hilly, undulating regions of the interior, which some people think take away from the otherwise ageless landscape. The way I look at it is everyone takes pictures of old windmills in Holland, so we just have to wait awhile before these ones become quaint and photogenic as well.

Jan and Roger had a guidebook with the usual cursory explanations and they asked me if I knew anything about the mosaics. I told them about the Pantocrator. The Pantocrator is the most impressive figure in the Palatine Chapel. It's found in the semi-dome of the apse and it's a figure common in Byzantine church decoration: Christ as 'Ruler of All'. He holds a Bible in one hand, open to the passage from John 8:12: "I am the light of the World. Whoever follows me will not walk in darkness, but will have the light of life." In this instance it's bilingual, with Latin on the right and Greek on the left, the languages of Catholicism and Orthodoxy respectively. Christ's hand gesture is a mudra of the very letters that float above his head on the left and right: IC and XC, a monogram for Christ's name (specifically, a 'Christogram', just in case you want to impress someone—does not refer to an e-mail from the pope), which in Greek is IHCOΥC XPICTOC The first and last letters from each name are taken as abbreviations. The sideways S-shaped line above the letters indicates the name is a holy one. That should be sufficient Orthodox epigraphy for you to intimidate, or bore to death, whomever you're travelling with.[11]

The Pantocrator's ominous, unblinking presence pervades the chapel, gazing upon all who enter; in the past worshippers, today throngs of tourists. Oddly, a figure depicted in resplendent mosaic cautions you to reject the world's sensuous pleasures in a medium that is itself a sensuous pleasure, thus embodying the irony of the icon and the idolatry of the aesthetic: the beautiful articulation of the vanity of beauty. Staring down this imposing image was the king himself, whose throne platform is at the opposite side of the church, with another image of Christ above him, flanked by the saints the chapel is dedicated to, Peter and Paul. One of Roger II's biographers, Alexander of Telese, noted that Peter and Paul were special guardians to Roger II, and Christ's presence hovering above the enthroned king would have augmented the notion of the divine blessing of Roger's rule.

It was before these two saints in the Palatine chapel, on November 20th of 1194, Peter of Eboli tells us, that the tragic Queen Sibylla kneeled in prayer when it became evident that the Holy Roman Emperor, Henry IV, would conquer Palermo. The citizens had capitulated to Henry and his German army, which was encamped at Favara just south of the city, very close to where the Norman Robert of Guiscard had stationed his troops when he besieged the city 123 years before. On December 25th, Christmas day, Henry was crowned king of Sicily in the Palermo cathedral. Young William III, the rightful heir to the throne, but only eight years old, was present at the coronation. Chroniclers record that he had to kneel at Henry's feet and submit to the usurper. Nobody knows what happened to the boy after that. Henry probably had him killed. As an even greater humiliation to the Norman line it is said that the tombs of the earlier kings were opened and their royal crowns and vestments plundered. Witnesses record that a huge train of horses took the treasures to Germany. Eventually Henry, too, would inhabit a porphyry sepulcher here in Palermo cathedral.

Noah makes appearances in the Palatine mosaics since, as seafarers, the Normans saw in him an appropriate parallel as it was by ships they'd come to this warm land—John Julius Norwich called it their 'kingdom in the sun'—and their navy was one of the most powerful in the Mediterranean.[12] It's hard not to think about the wealth of the Norman kings when looking at a monument like the Palatine Chapel. Numerous chroniclers described Sicily's incredible riches during the Norman period. As Ibn Jubayr, the Arab traveler who visited in 1184 put it, "the prosperity of the island surpasses description." Given what the chapel must have cost, it's hard to believe Romuald of Salerno's description of Roger II as "very careful in acquiring money, but not too generous in spending it." At least here he seems to have loosed the purse strings. The sumptuousness of the chapel accords with the finery of Roger's court, as visitors were "impressed to find the palace floors lined with multi-coloured carpets, the servants clad in silk, and food served on gold plates."

There's a remarkable artifact that survives from Roger's reign, a silk cloak he wore during ceremonial occasions. It's one of the most superb textiles ever created.[13] Pearls are sewn into the design, with elaborate stitching in golden thread. It could have been Roger's coronation mantle, though its date of 1133 CE makes it a bit early for that. Still, it gives a sense of the splendor of court ritual. Around the edges, in Arabic, are inscriptions which include phrases such as, "Here is what was created in the princely treasury, filled with good fortune, illustrations, majesty, perfection, longevity, superiority ... the pleasure of days and nights, without cease or change ... [made] in the capital of Sicily, in the year 528 H." The date 528 H. is a Muslim date. The 'H' stands for '*hejiri*' from the word '*hejira*' or 'flight', the zero year of the Islamic calendar, beginning from the Prophet Muhammad's flight from Mecca to Medina in our year 622 CE. So 528 equates with 1133 CE. The cloak has a half-moon shape, over eleven feet wide, and has fantastic golden lions attacking camels on a deep red silk background. Ironically, since the mantle was very likely made by Arab craftsmen, these animals represent the Catholic Normans' victory over the Muslims. It was one of the treasures looted by Henry and taken to Germanic lands, which is why you have to go to Vienna to see it today.

Near the Norman Palace is a little church that, like the Palatine Chapel, is an eloquent marker of Palermo's multicultural past: San Giovanni degli Eremiti (St John of the Hermits). The original, sixth-century church on the site was later converted, with substantial reconstruction, into a mosque in the Arab period (ca. 900-1070 CE), then made into a

Catholic church in the Norman era (ca. 1071-1194). So it served as a place of worship for three successive dynasties. So revered was this modest church that Roger II designated it as the official burial place for the high ranking courtiers of the palace and decreed that its priest would be the Confessor to the King, a post of no small esteem. It's hard to explain what it might be like to wander around in a Byzanto-Muslim-Norman-Catholic building, but if anyone at a cocktail party asked me what structure best represented this experience (I've been asked stranger things at cocktail parties), this might be the place I'd sent them.

When I left the chapel I realized I had time to go to the Palazzo Abatellis, one of Palermo's best museums. The fifteenth-century Palazzo Abatellis was almost completely destroyed in the Allied bombing of 1943. Stone by stone it was rebuilt to its original form. The work was completed in 1953 and it was designated the city's museum of medieval, renaissance, and baroque painting and sculpture. Most of the art is religious, but that's appropriate because the building had done service for centuries as a nunnery. It's a remarkable collection and nowhere else in Palermo can you get such a powerful sense of the city's artistic greatness from the fourteenth through the eighteenth centuries. The altarpieces alone are worth the visit.

Among the many masterpieces is the huge mid-fifteenth century mural of the *Triumph of Death*,

COMPLESSO MONUMENTALE
MONREALE
Santa Maria La Nuova

Monreale Compl.Monumentale Intero

Biglietti/Tickets: 1 - Tot. euro 12,00

Vale per 1 ingresso il/Valid for 1 entrance on: 24/09/2019

2019-09-24T11:08:04

1Y7EUHZ3AQ7HJ5

M:1011.103.190924.302

one of history's most dramatic visual embodiments of the horror of death and futility of human vanity. An apocalyptic skeleton streaks through the sky, riding a cadaverous horse larger than life and at full gallop, evoking a passage in the Book of Revelation: "I looked and beheld a pale horse: and the name of who sat on him was Death." The horse is an incomparable image of terror. I'm convinced Picasso saw it and recalled its head in his mural *Guernica*. On the right, young noblewomen in luxurious clothing relax in a garden while young men play music; but their idyllic grove of courtly love is at this very moment coming under the shadow of the merciless horseman. Below, the young and beautiful are felled by indiscriminate arrows that fly from Death's black bow, his quiver ever full. In one group a lavishly dressed woman is struck by two arrows, one in her neck and another in her breast. Ladies in waiting hold her as she collapses, looking on in horror as she breathes her last. Death has arrived so quickly she's barely had time to react. Her sumptuous golden necklace, fine clothes and earthly beauty offer no defense against the pitiless onslaught. Elsewhere kings, sultans, bishops and popes are also pierced by cruel darts. To the left the artist and his assistant calmly make eye contact with you, as if reminding you to take the message of the painting seriously. They are part of a group that Death's arrows have for the moment bypassed. These common people recognize Death, respect its power, and are thus for now spared. Old people and the poor, dressed in simple clothes, are foils to the youthful courtly lovers on the other side of the work, whose vanities are being ravaged by the grim reaper.

One of the museum's other masterworks is in every way the contrary of the *Triumph of Death*. It's small, still, peaceful and full of hope for salvation: Antonello da Messina's *Virgin Annunciate* of around 1460. The Annunciation has already happened and the angel Gabriel has departed. Only the glow of his angelic presence softly illuminates Mary from an invisible window to the left. She is alone in her room, left to ponder the momentousness of what has just occurred. She is bathed in divine light, and her magnificently foreshortened hand hovers over the Old Testament in which she has read the prophesy she has just experienced the fulfillment of. She is beautiful. She gazes off into space, yet she seems preternaturally conscious of her destiny. She modestly clasps her blue robe to her chest. Her hand gestures are delicate, and yet her face is that of a lovely Sicilian peasant girl, strong and determined, with wide cheek bones, yet with soft and sensuous lips. She's the most kissable Madonna in the history of art. She has fully submitted to the will of God and has the personal strength to do what has been asked of her. All of this Antonello conveys in this most simple of paintings. Not until da Vinci's *Mona Lisa* does an artist equal this enigmatic but powerful depiction of a lovely woman's face.

I broke my one-hour rule by a long shot; there were just too many riches in the Abatellis. When I finally left I thought I should see the spectacular unfinished church of Santa Maria dello Spasimo, which was nearby. It's Gothic in style, making you think it's from the Middle Ages, but in fact it was begun much later, in 1509, during the High Renaissance period. It has an odd name. The *spasimo* is a 'spasm', or, more correctly, a 'swooning'; in this case of the Virgin Mary. The monastery attached to the church commissioned a painting of the subject from none other than Raphael, showing the moment when Christ stumbles as he carries the cross and his mother suffers a shudder of pain, a '*spasimo*', at seeing him in such anguish. Raphael's painting had been on its way to Palermo after it was finished around 1516, but the ship floundered in a storm and sank. The painting was salvaged by the crew, however, who took it to Naples. There, someone assumed the Virgin didn't want to go to Palermo, seeing as how she'd whipped up the tempest that sank the ship, so the masterpiece was redirected by the Spanish Viceroy to Madrid, where it now hangs in the Prado.

More troubles were in store for the ill-fated monastery and church of the Spasimo. Threats to Sicily from the Ottoman Turks in the 1530s led to construction being abandoned. Cut stone was now needed for city walls and fortifications. The church was mostly completed, but its soaring nave vaults were never built. Now, one has the remarkable experience of being in a huge Gothic church completely open to the sky. Surreally, but also picturesquely, a tree has grown in a corner, its top branches now as high as the vaults would have been. A concert stage has been set up in the apse, where the altar and Raphael's painting were once destined to be. I made a note to attend a recital here in the future. It reminded me of Famagusta, on Cyprus, where many ruined churches are also open to the sky, their rib vaults long ago fallen. I wandered around in awe in that extraordinary space, the blue sky above with wispy clouds beginning to turn a mute tint of orange as the sun approached the horizon.

I walked back to the Casa Sicilia slowly. The shopkeepers in the Mercato del Capo along the Via Porta Carini were cleaning up and the cobbles were wet with fishy ice and the detritus of the day's fruits and vegetables. I bought some mortadella and cheese and an aluminum take-away container of pasta alla Norma from a fast food hole in the wall. I knew it was a good place because I had to elbow out pushy locals to get my order in. Set for dinner and ready for a night's sleep, I dragged myself back to the Casa Sicilia.

DAY FIVE

The more we see of Palermo, and the more minutely it is examined, the more we shall be sensible of its beauty. Handsome streets, large and beautiful squares, public fountains... superb churches, and delightful walks; a good air, a vast population, with a cleanliness not to be found in any other city of the kingdom.

-Jean Claude Richard de Saint Non, 1778

Morning

I slept well and set out the next morning, entering the Porta Carini and its scenic market at about 9:00 am. Vendors' cries projected like opera singers' arias, as fresh in the cool morning as their goods. There were no tourists and the locals were doing their shopping. In one of the fish stalls was an enormous Bluefin tuna, its flesh a deep blood red (the French simply call them *Thon Rouge*, 'Red Tuna'), owing to the extraordinarily high hemoglobin content of their blood, which facilitates oxygen uptake. While appreciating the unlikelihood of any circumstance in which I'd be compelled to hug a tuna, its girth was so great that I swear I couldn't have got my arms around it. I found out from a fisherman named Dario that these were illegal, since taking tuna was forbidden at this time of the month, which is why the numbers of tuna in the Mediterranean have decreased by about 80% in recent years. The World Wildlife Federation lists the Mediterranean / Atlantic Bluefin (*tunnus thynnus*) as an endangered species. Twenty-first century technologies and the use of spotting planes and sonars make it impossible for the large breeding fish to escape the nets. There's little enforcement at the retail end of the equation, it seems, because I saw such giants in other markets for several days in a row.

Inhabitants of Sicily have pursued the great tuna for millennia. The ancient Phoenicians and Romans fished for them off of Sicily's shores, but one can go even further back in history. On the island of Levanzo, the smallest of the three Egadi Islands, about ninety kilometers southeast of Palermo, is a cave known locally as the *Grotta del Genovese*, the walls of which are covered in prehistoric engravings and paintings, the latter dating from around 3000 BCE, the end of the Neolithic period. Among the other animals depicted on the cave's walls—such as a bull and dolphin—is the earliest known representation of a tuna.

The Bluefin is one of the most remarkable creatures of the sea. They're built for speed. Theresa Maggio writes, "...Bluefin sprint faster than torpedoes. The largest are as big as sports cars and can accelerate from zero to sixty in ten seconds—in water, a medium eight hundred times denser than air...

When the Bluefin hits top speed, their pelvic, pectoral, and front dorsal fins all retract into slots. They use ram ventilation, as do jet engines, swimming with their mouths open to get oxygen... They are superlative animals; their only predators are sharks, killer whales, and humans."

There's a legendary centuries-old Sicilian technique for catching these magnificent fish, in a series of enormous net traps—one over a mile long—eventually enclosed in by a flotilla of boats, its final manifestation called the *camera della morte* or 'chamber of death', where the fish are concentrated. The resulting mass of thrashing tuna, and the subsequent slaughter, is called the *mattanza*, a word that in Sicilian is a synonym for massacre. The fish are hauled into the boats by men with long poles with sturdy gaffs. Some of the fish are so large that it takes eight men to hoist them aboard. Officially, the *mattanza* doesn't happen anymore. The *mattanza* rose to the status of a religious ceremony for Sicilian fishermen, an annual ritual of violence akin to the Spanish bullfight, so deeply was the act woven with Sicilian life on the sea.

Even in the Middle Ages there was a well-developed tuna processing industry in Palermo. The salt industries of Trapani and Marsala del Vallo prospered partly in response to the need for salt for preserving fish. During the fishing seasons, especially at Lent, when the demand was high, and between May and July, when the fish ran, virtual cities appeared, entirely populated by *tonnaroti*, workers in the tuna industry. There were the fishermen, of course, but also butchers, salters, and packers. Certain special skills, such as pickling fish, were passed down from father to son. Jews were employed as roe salters, having expertise in this process. The demand for laborers, and a measure of the profits accrued, can be found in records that show wages doubled between 1328 and 1440. Some of the larger concerns caught 1000 tuna in a season, which is about 38 tons at a very respectable 760 pounds per fish (the modern record for a Bluefin is double that at 1497 pounds). Today, one of those huge medieval fish could sell for millions. In a record purchase in 2013 the Japanese sushi restaurant owner Kiyoshi Kimura paid $1,512,000 US for a 488 pound Bluefin. At that rate our average medieval Sicilian tuna would fetch a price of $2,354,708. The record Bluefin, at that price per pound, would have sold for $4,638,246.

At the Florio *tonnara* on Favignana—a remarkable industrial structure with 35,000 square meters of workspace, now a museum—there is a plaque that memorializes the record year of 1878 when 10,159 tuna were taken in a single season. Not far away, a statue of the Virgin Mary watches over Favignana. Instead of the infant Christ, she reverently cradles a tuna in her arms.

As I walked through the market I saw another stall where a magnificent swordfish, about seven feet long, was strung up like a puppet, caught as if fighting a line in mid-air leap. In front of it pools of gelatinous squid and octopi slumped in plastic tubs, their black eyes peering out of a jellied mass. Myriad creatures of the sea—sardines, snapper, shrimp, mackerel, tiny anchovies, crabs—were in abundance, arranged in trays of snowy ice.

I needed a cup of coffee so decided that this was the morning I would do something I'd been anticipating ever since I arrived. I was writing a book on Palermo so I reckoned I had to go to the famous Café Mazzara where Giuseppe di Lampedusa used to hang out while he was writing *The Leopard*. I was sure some literary genius would rub off on me. Alas, my hope of sipping coffee with a ghost of greatness was not to be. The Café Mazzara had been completely modernized and had none of the fin-de-siècle ambience I'd fantasized about. Anyway, it was closed because, as a sign taped on the window informed me, the workers were on strike. Those very workers were demonstrating nearby with a banner that read "Shame! Thirty-two Families out of Work. Bar Mazzara." Right beside me at that moment, as the strikers happily belted out a boisterous labour song, were the bronze doors of the Fascist-era Bank of Sicily. Fascist art focusses on workers, as did the realist art of socialism and the social realism of American public art in the 1930s.

So there before me were two commentaries on labor: to my left the picketing personnel of the Café Mazzara and to the right the doors of the Bank of Sicily showing rigid proletarians mechanically tackling their heroic tasks, building boats in shipyards and fishing for tuna. Above are scenes of family life where father and mother do their gender-specific duties; mum cares for the child while dad does some carpentry. In one of the more macabre panels two doctors dissect cadavers in a bizarre Dr. Mengele scene. There was a relief of worker bees above the doors and I realized that I should go inside and see if there was any more art there. I went in and, sure enough, there were lots of interesting reliefs. Some were created by a Palermitan sculptor who was known as a designer of medals and coins, which explained the lucid, shallow relief. His name was Filippo Sgarlata (b. 1901, d. 1979). If you're from Providence, Rhode Island, go down to Garibaldi Square in Federal Hill and you'll see a bust of Garibaldi done by Sgarlata in the late 1920s. The other reliefs were done by a sculptor named Giovanni Rosone (b. 1910, d. 2001), also from Palermo. Here, too, especially in Rosone's reliefs, labour was celebrated, although apparently it's best to do it in the nude since the workers were all naked or close to it. In one muscled men hauled in huge tuna in a *mattanza*. There were more bees, low down on one of the piers, working alongside ants with an inscription in Latin saying something along the lines of "careful bees and small ants are [good] examples". Examples of good workers I guess. Strangely, the ceiling of the bank had hexagonal designs that made the whole place look like a beehive. I looked at the bank employees buzzing about in their expensive Italian suits. Astonishingly, one had a black jacket and a yellow shirt, completing the metaphor with a flourish.[14]

Another inscription, this one above a relief of a sad looking young man and woman, reads 'They who sow tears shall reap joy'. It encourages people to accept exploitation and abuse from the rich and powerful now for the promise of rewards after you're dead. Amazing how many people through history have fallen for that. It was chilling, in a way, and made me wonder if the management of the Café Mazzara thought of their employees as insects who should toil away like drones. When I went out I tossed a couple of Euros into the workers' strike fund hat and got an enthusiastic cheer. I would've preferred leaving a tip after a cappuccino at the Mazzara, with the benevolent spirit of Giuseppe di Lampedusa guiding my hand as I took inspired notes on a napkin with the café's logo on it.

Palermo has lots of Fascist architecture that's worth seeing. Mussolini's state architects constructed numerous buildings in Palermo and other Italian provincial capitals from the late 1920s and through the 1930s as part of public works projects to lower unemployment. The same thing happened in the U. S. as the government tried to deal with the displacement and poverty caused by the Great Depression. Some of these structures are cold, austere blocks, like Palermo's Central Post office, built in 1928-35 by the architect Angelo Mazzoni. It's elevated on a huge platform like a Roman temple, but really wide, so you have to go up its broad staircase with colossal white columns looming over you. All of this intimidation just to get some stamps? At the top corners of the facade are flying victory figures, imparting, I suppose, that the mail or telegraphs will be delivered quickly. Tucked off to the south side of the building is a statue of St Christopher carrying the infant Christ by the sculptor Benedetto de Lisi. It's not exactly common to see religious imagery in Fascist art. The only justification that seemed reasonable was that St Christopher, because he was strong, fit the idea of Fascist manhood, and that carrying Christ (the name literally means 'Christ Bearer' in Greek) was meant to parallel the postal delivery man's duty to bear his heavy mail bags through all weather.

The main interior room of the post office is worth looking into. It's like an enormous cavern with huge vaults that imitate those of an imperial Roman bath complex. But the *pieces de résistance* are the magnificent murals in the building's meeting room, painted by the Futurist artist Benedetta Cappa (she preferred to be known only as 'Benedetta'), the wife of the founder of the Futurist artistic movement, Marinetti. The huge paintings were done for the room in 1933-34. The series was called

'Synthesis of Communications', befitting the Post Office's roles not only in mail but telegraph and radio communications, all done in shades of blue. If you're a New Yorker, you might have been lucky enough to see them in 2014 as part of a show on Italian Futurism at the Guggenheim. It was the first time the paintings had ever been out of the Palermo Post Office.

Another uninspiring Fascist pile in Palermo is the Palazzo di Giustizia (Palace of Justice), designed by the architects Ernesto and Gaetano Rapisardi. It was begun in 1938 but not finished until well after the war in 1957. The Piazza Vittorio Emanuele Orlando in front of it is a vacant piazza much in need of trees and benches, but if all you want to do is kick a soccer ball around or learn to ride a bike then it's a great place. In truth, that piazza had security more than civic convenience in mind, and given the ruptures of mafia violence through history it's no wonder. So many mafiosi cycled through the building's doors that it became known as the *Palazzo dei Veleni*, the 'Palace of Poisons'.

There are two much more attractive examples of Fascist design close to the Teatro Massimo. One is a monument, like an open air altar, known rather grimly as the Casa del Mutilato (1938), which was designed by the architect Giuseppe Spatrisano. It was constructed as a memorial to the dead of Italy's First World War struggle against the Austro-Hungarians, who had long dominated the north-eastern parts of Italy, but it's also a memorial to all veterans who'd been killed or maimed, hence the *mutilato* (above the west door is the original sign: *Associazione Mutilati e Invalidi di Guerra*: 'Association of War Amputees and Handicapped'). The west side of the building has offices for what in America might be called the Veteran's Administration, dealing with cases of wounded soldiers. Two large reliefs flank the façade, one a seated personification of Italy with sword in hand ready to defend the nation, and the other a winged victory that carries an olive branch of peace. There's a touching epigraph on the west side of the building, *Il Nostro Spirito e Luce che non se spegne* ('Our Spirit and Light are not Extinguished'), while on the east side there's the inscription *Fu seme il fante e la vittoria il fiore* (The Soldier was the Seed and Victory was the Flower'). I don't usually like war memorials but I thought that this building fused the war memorial and administrative building together in an interesting and successful way. They let me in to see the interior, and the doors and brass work were all original, along with some much damaged and depressing murals of the battlefield in the portico, which has an impressive circular oculus above, open to the sky.

My favorite example of Fascist architecture in Palermo is right next door, the central administrative building of the Sicilian Vigili del Fuoco (Firefighters Building) by the architect Antonio Pollaci. Rarely do Fascist structures exhibit so much style and color. It's a fine building and still used today as the Sicilian firefighters head office. The main gate is usually open so you can see the internal courtyard filled with red fire trucks. There's a plaque on the wall commemorating fallen firefighters. The dates on buildings of this period often have two numbers, like one here that says MCMXXIX, which is 1929, followed by another date, VIII E. F. What this latter date means is year 8 of the *Era Fascista*. Mussolini thought he'd instigated such a wonderful new age that using the old calendar years was passé, so he decided to start it running again from a new year one, 1921, the year of the birth of Italian Fascism. Books published in those years also have *E. F.* publication dates.

Just as the Fascist arts of Palermo tend to get ignored by tour groups who breeze too hastily through the Palatine Chapel on their way to Monreale, so, too, are the wonderful nineteenth-century Art Nouveau buildings. In Italy the Art Nouveau style is known as the *Stile Liberty* or Liberty Style, a designation also used in England. It has nothing to do with freedom. In England the name was derived from Arthur Lasenby Liberty, who in 1875 built the Liberty Department Store on Regent Street in London in the new style. The Liberty Style is all flow and curves, inspired by the idea that there are no straight lines in nature. In the 1890s, Palermo's golden age, the city was called 'The Little Capital of Art Nouveau', so rich with wonderful buildings it was. Despite wartime bombings and the predations of greedy, demolition-minded mafia contractors the city still has a surprisingly rich assortment of late-nineteenth and early-twentieth-century masterpieces such as the Villa Dato with its organic, flowing window frames, designed by Vincenzo Alagna in 1901, and the two kiosks of the Tabacchi Ribaudo. There's one of the latter near the front of the Teatro Massimo, where it's joined by the Tabacchi Rivendita—which was inspired by Japanese architecture—and another in the Piazza Castelnuovo. There are also some great apartment buildings, a few of which are in the neighborhood around the former house of Palermo's greatest practitioner of the style, Ernesto Basile (1857-1932).

Basile was Palermo's most accomplished architect, following his father in the profession. He was born and died in the city, though he taught for years at the University of Rome. It might have been witnessing the first examples of Fascist architecture being built that killed him in 1932, and it's probably a good thing since then he didn't also have to see some of his villas being destroyed by bombs in 1943 in the allied push through Sicily. Basile was the final project architect of the Teatro Massimo, the city's grandest edifice, though the building was originally designed by his father. It was Basile who created the aforementioned Ribaudo Tabacci kiosks and many other remarkable buildings around the city, a good number of which survive.

Basile played ingeniously with the city's architectural past: Arab, Norman, Renaissance, Baroque, and updated them to a new synthesis in the spirit of Liberty / Art Nouveau. His splendid house, the Villino Ida (Via Siracusa, 15) built in 1904, has all the components you could ask for: elegant ironwork, woodwork, ceramic tiles, mosaic flooring, painted decorations, stained glass... the works. Over the main door is a mosaic inscription that sums up Palermo, *DISPAR ET UNUM*, or "Diversity and Unity".

One of Basile's greatest masterpieces is the Villa Igiea, today The Grand Hotel Villa Igiea. The original *palazzo* on the site was built for an English Admiral at the end of the eighteenth century, but the property was later purchased by Ignazio Florio, who owned a profitable tuna-processing concern. You can still visit the Florio Tonnara on the island of Favignano just a few kilometers off the Sicilian coast between Trapani and Marsala. The huge complex was designed by Giuseppe Damiani Almeyda, the architect of Palermo's wonderful Teatro Politeama Garibaldi. Ignazio Florio's father, Vincenzo, also began the production of Marsala wine in 1832 and you can still visit the Florio winery in Marsala and taste the vintages. That venture, too, added to the family's considerable fortunes. Ignazio Florio hired Basile in 1899 to reconstruct and enlarge the earlier villa and he named it 'Igiea' after his daughter, who herself was named after Hygieia, the Greek goddess of sanitation and health (appropriately, that goddess's father was Asclepius, the god of medicine). We get our word 'hygiene' from her.

There's a wonderful photograph of the Florio family in an early automobile, showing Ignazio and his wife, Franca, with little Igiea in the front seat.[15] Mom's driving. Franca Florio also makes a dramatic appearance in a terrific 1924 portrait by Giovanni Boldini, who was known as 'the master of swish' for his elegant, curving figures and brush strokes. She wears a black dress and shows off her famous necklace of 365 pearls, one for every day of the year. It's very flattering, though the painting was done when she was 51 years of age. An 1899 photograph of Franca from twenty years earlier shows that even then, at the age of 26, she wasn't quite that ravishing. In other family gossip Franca's husband, Ignazio, is thought to have had an affair with Beatrice Palma, the mother of Giuseppe di Lampedusa, the author of *The Leopard*. This wasn't an isolated incident. It's said that every time Franca found out about one of her husband's indiscretions he assuaged her with gifts of extravagant jewelry. In her old age she had about thirty kilos of it. The Florios were Palermo's first and wealthiest family at the turn of the century, hosting the city's brief *belle epoch* from the 1880s to 1908, after which the family's fortunes collapsed and Palermo's economy disintegrated with them. During that golden age people referred to Palermo as 'Floriopolis'.

The Villa Igiea is a wonderful building, situated by the sea and under the heights of Monte Pellegrino. It's beside the north marina, the Porto del' Aquasanta, so the well-heeled can moor their yachts and walk to the hotel. Nineteenth-century photographs show it as a lonely spot where local boys went swimming, with only one or two tiny fishing boats drawn up on shore. The entrance that faces the street isn't that impressive, but the sea façade is spectacular, with beautiful gardens and terrace restaurants. Beside the pool are stone columns reminiscent of Greek ruins, one of the hotel's iconic spots where the rich and famous would have their pictures taken. One ballroom, the size of a basketball court, dramatically conveys Basile's genius; today it's simply called the Basile Room. There's a remarkable chandelier running along the spine of the ceiling, with graceful metalwork and leaves made of glass. The wall paintings, by the Art Nouveau painter Ettore de Maria Bergler, depict a paradise of beautiful women who wear nothing but lingerie, more or less, as if from a monumental nineteenth-century Victoria's Secret catalog. They frolic with swans in a sunny glade, amidst trees heavy with fruit, fields of lilies, irises, poppies, and all kinds of flowers blooming in riotous fecundity. Their breasts swell like ripe pears, tipped with nipples tinted in pomegranate pink. Exquisite though they are, it's the ceiling that's the most impressive element, with slats like the ribs of a ship's hull except more curvaceous and organic.

It was nice of the concierge to let me wander around and look at all these things. Of course I'd told him, with dead seriousness, that I was Finland's foremost expert on Basile. Walking in the seaside gardens I saw a man in a white bathrobe on a balcony overlooking the sea. He was having tea, basking in the sun and enjoying the vista from his luxurious hotel room. He must have been a real estate mogul, an industrialist, a CEO, a banker, a Persian Gulf sheikh … certainly he wasn't a travel writer. Well, I guess it could've been Bryson. I wondered if he was going to finish his croissant.

While Basile was working on the Villa Igiea he was also designing a smaller and more private suburban *villino* for Ignazio Florio, now known as the Villa Florio all'Olivuzza (built 1899-1903) on the Viale Regina Margherita just a five-minute walk north of La Zisa. This villa once had large gardens and artificial lake, now gone, though there's still a little park with trees. The Villa Florio almost became one of Basile's tragic architectural fatalities, not from wartime bombs but from a catastrophic fire in November of 1962. Though much damaged, the villa was beautifully restored. Another Basile survivor is the Villino Favaloro di Stefano in the Piazza Virgilio, which, like the Teatro Massimo, was begun by the elder Basile and finished by Ernesto in 1914. It was damaged in an earthquake in 2002, and since then has lain forlornly abandoned on its lot. It's one of dozens of Palermo's masterpieces that are in limbo, with insufficient funding for restoration.

Afternoon

Walking back from the Villa Igiea I took a little detour and went by the imposing walls and fences of the infamous Ucciardone prison (also affectionately known as 'The Mafia Hotel') first built in 1830 by the repressive French Bourbon regime but, amazingly, still functioning today. I could see the modern Aula Bunker where the so-called Maxi Trial (*Maxiprocesso*) was held in 1986-87, where over four hundred mafiosi were tried. This high security courtroom was built specifically for those famous hearings, right on the jailhouse grounds so prisoners could be moved from cells to courtroom without transport through city streets. Double, backup judges were assigned to all cases, since it was so likely that one of them would be murdered. I wanted to see the inside of the courtroom, but they told me I needed authorization, though they also told me it was visiting hours and if I knew an inmate I could visit him. I walked away and then realized I should have said I wanted to see Giovanni, just to see what happened. It might've been interesting, or fatal. When I got to the Via Libertà I took the 101 bus, the most useful line in the city, to the Quattro Canti and wandered for a while through the narrow streets of the Albergheria quarter. I didn't know what to do, so I pulled up on a bench and took out my map. I was a bit tired of the busy streets and when that happens I look for green patches. I saw a big one labeled 'Villa Trabia'.

If you want to get an authentic sense of how the eighteenth and nineteenth century Palermitan nobility lived with their vast estate gardens it's hard to match the Villa Trabia, its grounds having been turned into a city park, a miraculous survivor of the Sack of Palermo. It's one of the most relaxing places in the city. Tourists rarely go there, if the stares I'm getting are anything to go by. It gets its name from the estate of one of its early owners, Giuseppe Lanza Branciforte, who purchased it in 1814 and who was the prince of Trabia, which is about thirty kilometers southeast of Palermo. The groves of immense Moreton Bay figs are its most impressive horticultural features, but it's also remarkable that some of the original marble benches survive. Naturally, the youth of Palermo, quick on the draw with their felt pens, have marked these up with every possible juvenile commentary. I wish they'd keep to texting.

The fountains of the Villa Trabia have run dry. One, in the carriage court of the villa, has had a pine tree in it for over fifty years. Nobody saw fit to remove it and now its roots have completely enveloped the fountain, which has essentially ceased to exist. Those same roots are now dismantling the wall in which the erstwhile fountain was ensconced. Elsewhere a statue of an oceanic triton, which once blew water from his conch shell, is now landlocked and silent, his gurgling sea fountain turned into an arid terrestrial planter. Ivy, green against his white marble skin, spirals around his torso instead of seaweed.

I found terrific greenhouses that seemed to be from the 19th or early 20th century, with wonderful ironwork frames. I entered one and a woman told me it was forbidden to look inside. I looked at her quizzically and left, not wanting to argue about it. My grandfather was a nurseryman and I have many fond memories of playing as a child in his greenhouse in Chilliwack, British Columbia. It was especially marvelous in the dead of winter. With snow piled up outside I could go into that unlikely tropical garden with cacti and orchids blooming, the whole thing heated by a small cast iron stove. The Villa Trabia gardens are a bit sparse now, but they must have been resplendent in the old days, with paths trimmed with colorful blooms. I sat and read for a while and wrote notes in my journal.

Later, returning to the Casa Sicilia along the Via Carini, doing some shopping for dinner, I glanced up a nondescript alleyway that had nothing at all of interest in it. Yet I hesitated, I'm not sure why. It may be that over the years I've developed a nose for things and, sure enough, in that derelict lane was a masterpiece. Palermo has some of the most impressive mosaics in the world: the Palatine Chapel, Monreale, and the Church of the Admiral. These are the incomparable treasures the city is famous for, and yet in this alleyway, exquisite but neglected, with garbage cans lying in front of it, is one of Palermo's most beautiful works of art: an Art Nouveau Ceres in the façade of the *Panificio of Salvatore Morello*. If you're from Chicago you've seen a version of the goddess Ceres in the 30-foot aluminum statue atop the Chicago Board of Trade building, built in 1930. In Sicily Ceres symbolized the island's grain production just as her Chicago sister designated the American capital of Midwestern wheat production. The Statue of Liberty in New York is a cousin, in a way, because Ceres (Demeter to the Romans) eventually became associated with the concept of democracy and freedom from tyranny. When Sicilians arrived at Ellis Island that towering figure would have been both welcoming and familiar, since according to mythology Ceres lived in Sicily. Interestingly, the statue was dedicated in 1886, at the start of mass Sicilian immigration to America. It was Ceres' daughter, Persephone, who was abducted by Pluto and, accordingly, her annual departure to Hades and her return to the upper world produce the seasons of winter and spring.

The mosaic Ceres I was admiring was commissioned by the original proprietor of the now defunct bakery, Salvatore Morello, from another Salvatore, Salvatore Gregoretti. It reminded me of the paintings of Gustav Klimt, who himself took inspiration from Byzantine mosaics. Its color and design were remarkable. In any other city this would be a prized jewel in the city's most important museum.

Alas, in Palermo, this Art Nouveau tour de force hangs on the wall of a condemned building with nothing protecting it from vandalism or the elements. She has already lost several toes, and some of the glass has been shattered, perhaps by indifferent schoolboys throwing stones.[16]

This *fin de siècle* Ceres, who I suppose is a *début de siècle* Ceres since she was made in 1908, stands in her bare feet amidst a verdant glade with leaves of fleshy succulents sprouting from the pebbles of an undulating stream. She inhabits a verdant paradise, an orchard of springtime fertility, like an Art Nouveau version of the personification of spring in Botticelli's famous *Primavera.* She reaches up with pale slender arms into a luxuriant canopy of golden wheat interspersed with marvelous purple fruits that echo her amethyst earrings. Her robes splay in a fan of elegant pleats, bejeweled and sparkling, with a collar of lapis lazuli and a rainbow of hems. Inlaid slabs of opalescent alabaster form a ribboning backdrop for a cascade of dangling ropes playfully dotted with ornaments, and her severe classical profile shows the same passivity as the Greek goddesses in the Selinunte sculptures in Palermo's archeological museum. I sat on some steps in front of it, amazed to find this gem amongst the detritus of one of Palermo's most derelict alleyways. It seemed to me that the city is taking its chances neglecting this wonder, tempting the wrath of a powerful goddess, like the penny-pinching Selinuntians 2500 years ago. Gold leaf persists on some of the tesserae of the mosaic, having miraculously survived a price of $1900.00 an ounce in 2012.

I had a hot shower after dinner and went to bed early. It was only 8:45, but I was exhausted. Sometime around midnight I was awoken by deep rumbles and mute flickers, which in minutes became terrific explosions and bright flashes. For the longest time the tempest growled dry, the desiccated taste of static on the air, but finally the rain erupted from the black sky and assailed the rooftops with slashing talons. Soon the building's troughs were gargling loudly as torrents rushed down their throats. The rain calmed me, though, reminding me of my childhood home. I slid easily to sleep again and dreamt as great dark clouds rushed onwards to Sardinia on the back of a fierce African wind.

DAY SIX

I suppose that Palermo, the great Bay of Palermo with its lofty promontories thrust out into the sea, so noble in outline and in mass, Monte Pellegrino in the west and Monte Alfano on the east, the city set as it were in a natural amphitheater between them on the jewel-like sea [and] the Conca d'Oro… with its olive gardens, its orange and lemon groves, its fig trees and almonds…I suppose Palermo is one of the loveliest places in the world.

-Edward Hutton, *Cities of Sicily*, 1926

Morning

Believe it or not, there were still medieval churches in Palermo I hadn't seen. One was dedicated to Mary Magdalene and the other was known as the Magione church or Santa Trinita. The first is close to the Norman palace and few people see it because it doesn't appear on most tourist maps and it's not so easy to get into. It was probably built around 1140, early in Roger II's reign. It's tiny, but of quintessentially Norman design: stark, blockish, with a single apse. The reason it's hard to visit is because it's in an enclosed area where the head offices of the *Caribinieri* (state police) for Sicily are located. In the eighteenth century, during

Spanish rule, the area was a military garrison, and that military function has continued today as the *Caribinieri* headquarters, named after Carlo Alberto della Chiesa, the *Caribinieri* chief who was assassinated by the mafia in 1982.

The entrance is on the north side of the Corso Vittorio Emanuele just before you get to the Porta Nuova. As you enter, just to your right is an office that usually has two *Caribinieri* in it. You need to convince one of them to take you in, which is not always an easy thing to do. I suggest showing up at about 10:00 am with two take-away coffees and a couple of cannoli. I was turned away the first time I went. The reason was, as one officer muttered after the other walked outside, that his partner "was a bit of a shit-head", if I got the idiom right, and I should come back tomorrow when he wasn't working. Anyway, I was coming back now and a new pair was on guard. I'd figured that if I walked up and confidently stated in perfect Italian that I wanted to see the Church of Mary Magdalene and that I was an expert on the Norman architecture of Palermo they might react to my self-assurance and fluency by immediately granting me access.

I rehearsed my phrases over and over again as I walked towards the Porta Nuova, perfecting every nuance. One of the guards was out on the sidewalk just in front of the entrance. I approached him, perfect Italian at the tip of my tongue. He turned as I approached and, of course, I was immediately intimidated by the immaculate and decidedly Fascist *Caribinieri* uniform and blurted out something that probably sounded like a request for him to spank my sister. Thank god it didn't sound like I wanted to spank his sister. I'd still be in lock-up today. After my nonsensical flurry he raised one substantial eyebrow, the way Mr. Spock used to do when Doctor McCoy said something idiotic on Star Trek, but I guess he decided that my Italian was the best entertainment he was going to get all day so he nodded and took me to the church, which, for the love of god is just fifteen meters inside the main gate. He followed me everywhere and was very patient as I took my pictures and got out of there as soon as I could. He nodded an appreciation for my paramilitary promptness.

It was a hike to the next church, the Magione, but the walk was a scenic one through some engaging little alleys of the old city—through Palermo's poorest quarter, mostly inhabited by Indian, Bangladeshi and African immigrants—in the streets east of the Piazza del Carmine, through which the vivacious and curving ribbon of the Mercato Ballarò passes. A couple of the streets had streamers with pink and black pennants hanging across them, the colors of the Palermo football team, thus their nickname *Rosa-nero* ('Pink-Black', though they're also known as the *Aquile,* 'Eagles'). It might seem odd for a men's sports team to have pink as one of its colors but it's related to Santa Rosalia, whose symbol, logically, is the rose. A big playoff game with Catania FC was coming up; a fierce cross-island rivalry. I was getting a sore throat, so asked someone where a pharmacy was. In Palermo there's never one far away. Indeed, Italy in general seems a country of pharmacies. There's a story in there somewhere. There was one on the Via Vetriera, where I got some medicated lozenges.

I sat down on a bench in the sparse Piazza Magione and snacked on some bread and cheese I'd bought in the Ballerò. I saw boys playing football and I recalled something I'd read a few months before. This piazza is where Paolo Borsellino and Giovanni Falcone—who were both from this neighborhood, the Kalsa quarter—used to play as boys. Both grew up to be legendary anti-mafia prosecutors, and both were assassinated by the Corleonesi mafia in 1992. If you go to Palermo by plane you land in the airport named after them. Later, when I came home and was doing further research, I found out that Borsellino's mother had run that same pharmacy where I'd bought my throat lozenges, and that the Borsellino house had been right next door. Unwittingly, I'd shopped at a place of pilgrimage, one of the many sites related to the lives and deaths of Palermo's most excellent corpses or '*cadaveri eccelenti*', the name given to assassinated anti-mafia crusaders.

This district, the Kalsa, sustained heavy damage in the Allied bombing in 1943 when Borsellino and Falcone were about five years old. It must have been terrifying for a child, though perhaps from that experience they learned to control their fear, steeling them for the courageous struggle they would wage as adults. There are photographs showing the Magione church with its roof blown off. In the center of the Piazza Magione, as late as 1990, was a huge water tank as local residents didn't have plumbing, the neighborhood still suffering from the bombings forty-seven years before.

I entered the Magione's walled enclosure through the baroque gateway, which is such a contrast to the asceticism of the medieval church's façade. The Magione is small and simple, like San Giovanni dei Lebbrosi and the Magdalene church. They're all small, thick-walled and clunky compared to Gothic churches, but I appreciate their human scale and simplicity, which for me accords better with the austerity of Christ's example. The Magione was built by Matthew of Aiello (d. 1160), the Emir (*Ammiraglio*) of the royal court during the reign of King William II. I sat down in the church pews and took a load off my feet. In the late 18th century I wouldn't have been able to do that. The German traveler Joseph Hager noted in 1796 that "Certain whimsical customs also prevail in their churches. As chairs have not yet been introduced you must at your entrance hire a seat of straw, unless you would stand for the whole service. For this purpose poor ragged women are always to be found there, who provide you with them for money." I was glad I didn't have to buy a bale of hay, though I suppose I could've made fast friends of the carriage horses in town.

In the south chapel there was a painting of Mary nursing the infant Christ, but it looked like it was badly damaged. I wondered if it had been in the church when it was bombed. I imagined people going through the debris and triumphantly pulling the icon from the rubble and everyone around falling to their knees and proclaiming a miracle.

I was getting hungry so I walked over to the Via Roma and had lunch in a busy little café full of locals, its popularity a good barometer of its value. It was a typical fast-food place with great homemade dishes. The round tables were so small I had to do some creative folding with my map, which became a handy tablecloth. I had a delicious rice and cheese arancine the size of a baseball. I could barely finish it. After lunch and a macchiato I continued north along the Via Roma. I wanted to see the imposing nineteenth-century Cassa di Risparmio designed by Ernesto Basile. It's a grand building, with renaissance styling seasoned with virtuoso Art Nouveau details in stone and ironwork. The officious facades of the Fascist-era Bank of Sicily on the opposite side of the piazza provided a lesson in contrasting architectural styles.

The Cassa di Risparmio, like the Villa Igiea, is a fancy hotel nowadays. I snuck in through a side door to the restaurant and sheepishly asked if I could see the courtyard. The lone waiter let me cut through as a rather strange looking family ate lunch. They were the only people in the vast dining hall and it was kind of peculiar. It was a couple with their little boy and girl. All were dressed in clothes that suggested a formal event taking place in some bygone age. They sat in eerie silence in this huge, elegant ballroom. I skittishly traversed the floor beside this Felliniesque tableau, nodded to them nervously, took my pictures, and hightailed it out of there before things got even more surreal, like the corpses from the Capuchin cemetery suddenly materializing and waltzing across the parquetry floor. The place was beautiful but sort of creepy, like the off-season hotel in *The Shining*. In fact, the little girl was dressed just like the ghostly twins and had the same hair style too. I was worried she'd abruptly appear at my side from across the room and ask me if I wanted to play in an echoing voice. If anyone even remotely resembling Jack Nicholson walked in I would have run screaming into the street.

The Martorana was a five-minute walk away via the crooked alley called the Discesa dei Giudici or 'Decision of the Judges'. The street gets its name from the judges and law courts of the Corte Pretoriana, which it once led to. However, while that's undoubtedly a reasonable explanation for the thoroughfare's designation there's a more colorful story that claims the street gets its name from some judges during Spanish rule who were executed for corruption. Their corpses were displayed along this road and, later, their skin was used to make carpets that subsequent judges had to walk on as they entered chambers as a reminder to deliver honest legal decisions. I chased from my mind scenarios involving one or two of the Supreme Court justices.

When I came to the Piazza Bellini, over which both the Martorana and San Cataldo stand, there were school groups filing in so I decided to avoid the crowd and go to the nearby Fontana Pretoria. The fountain is huge, round in plan, with dozens of statues of gods, goddesses, nymphs, and allegorical figures, most of them stark naked. This is why people called it the *Fontana della Vergogna* or 'Fountain of Shame' when it was first erected in the late sixteenth century. The nudity was an issue for the nuns who lived in the convent of Santa Caterina that overlooks the piazza, but I bet they stole an appreciative peek every now and again. I have historical evidence for that cheeky and sacrilegious assertion. In 1796 Hager noted about the nuns of Palermo: "In other places they are usually confined for life; but in Palermo, youthful nuns are seen in carriages or, under the pretext of indisposition, in the houses of their relations. There they stand in the balconies over the streets, dressed in the habits of their order, [they] contemplate the youthful of the other sex, and frequently enter into lively and even gallant conversation ... I saw several married women in Palermo, who had been formerly nuns, and from the cloister had passed to the marriage bed." He also observed that the main reason the upper classes sent their daughters to nunneries was not so that they could dedicate their lives to God but "to guard against seduction," that is, to preserve their virginity until they came of marriageable age. Indeed, he notes that many were "married from the cloister, at the age of twelve, and become grandmothers at thirty." A related observation had been made twenty six years earlier by Brydone: "The Sicilian ladies marry at thirteen or fourteen, and are sometimes grandmothers before they are thirty. The Count Stetela presented us a few days ago to his cousin, the Princess Partana, who he told us had a great number of children, the eldest of which was a very fine girl of fifteen. We talked to the princess for half an hour, not in the least doubting all the time that she was the daughter, till at last the young lady came in; and even then, it was not easy to say which appeared the handsomest or the youngest. This lady has had twelve children and is still in her bloom." Sicilian women were often observed to have more interesting sex lives than women in northern European countries. In 1791 Brian Hill noted that "the crime of adultery is so common, that no Dame of rank is thought the worse of for being guilty of it."

Like the convent church, Palermo's city hall also overlooks the Fontana Pretoria, with the balcony from which it is said the victorious Garibaldi addressed the citizens of Palermo after taking the city in 1860.[17] The Fontana Pretoria was the masterwork of the Florentine sculptor Francesco Camilliani, who designed his aquatic wonder around 1550. It was praised by none other than the famous biographer of renaissance artists, Giorgio Vasari. John Dryden saw it in 1700 and was very impressed, though in his enthusiasm he incorrectly attributes one of the statues to Michelangelo, though one can hardly blame him because its head is reminiscent of the famous Moses in San Pietro in Vincoli: "...this fountain is very noble, and adorned with a great quantity of excellent statues, all in marble, and done by great masters; among these there is a Selinus by Michael Angelo Buonarota, in a lying posture... [they] equal those of antiquity."

The circular fountain is divided into four sections, marked by statues of recumbent old bearded men, allegories of Palermo's four ancient rivers: the Oreto, Maredolce, Papireto, and Gabriele. The goddess Venus (Aphrodite) stands nude, wearing only a necklace and crown and holding the golden apple awarded her by the handsome Trojan prince, Paris, who tragically judged her the most beautiful of the goddesses, thus precipitating the Trojan War. She's had a rough time of it, having made at least a couple of trips to the emergency ward. Her ankles and knees show she's broken apart on both those weak joints, probably in earthquakes, and she's needed marble patches on her left calf and right ankle. Her left hand must have snapped off in one of the falls and it had to be replaced with a new one. In fact, many of the figures have had parts broken off and clumsily repaired. Part of the explanation for the breakage—as well as the racy subject matter more suitable for private rather than public delectation—is that the fountain had originally been made for a Florentine patron, Luigi Alvarez de Toledo, the brother-in-law of Cosimo I de' Medici, who installed it in his Tuscan villa garden but later sold the whole thing to his brother, Don Garcia, the Spanish Viceroy in Palermo.[18] Thus this vast ensemble had to be disassembled, purportedly into 644 pieces, shipped by sea, and reassembled in its present location in front of the city's main governmental building.

I walked over to San Cataldo, right beside the Martorana, and from a terrace took some pictures of the gracefully curving dome of the church of San Giuseppe de Teatini with its zig-zag design of ceramic tiles in yellow and green. Parts of the church were looking a bit worse for wear. There weren't any school groups in San Cataldo, so I went in. San Cataldo was, like the Martorana, essentially a private chapel for an adjoining palace. It was built by Maio of Bari, another of the successors of George of Antioch—the builder of the Martorana next door—in the office of *Amir* or *Ammiraglio*. Maio held the position under King William I (The Not So Bad) from 1154 to his murder in November of 1160. San Cataldo gains much by occupying a raised platform overlooking the Piazza Bellini below, as the added elevation helps confer a degree of monumentality the building wouldn't otherwise have. Quite similar to most of the Norman churches in Palermo, this one is also a study in simplicity; a relatively unadorned rectangle with three domes on top.

The door was open and a curtain was hung in front of it, ballooning lightly in the breeze. On the other side two teenage girls conferred at a small ticket desk, keeping each other company and chatting *sotto voce* while tourists sauntered in a slow waltz punctuated with snapshots and selfies. Part of the church was cordoned off while two men worked on restoring some of the floor mosaics. They ground out the old cement with a tool like a dentist's drill and brushed out the powder, carefully extracting the triangles of colored stone, rinsing them in a bucket and arranging them on a drying cloth. They worked under bright lights on tripods. Their hair was dusted with cement powder—one, with curly hair, looked like he had a radiant halo—and with their protective eyewear and heavy canvas aprons they resembled miners. I tried to shut out the occasional buzz of their grinders.

The interior is starkly geometric, mysterious and dark, evoking medieval ceremonies from an age when devotion was grim and somber; with druidic liturgies illuminated by vague, trembling oil lamps. I imagined deep plainsong chants sounding off the stone walls and circulating up the domes, bearing the opulent smoke of frankincense in an ascending spiral. The tapping of the workman's mallet diverted me while the teenagers at the desk developed a case of the giggles. Real life, always chaotic and improvised, never ceremonial and measured, is the best religion of all. I'll take the laughter of the girls and the growl of the workman's tools over the incanting of priests any day.

The builder of San Cataldo, Maio of Bari, was either a tragic figure or a nasty fellow, depending on who you believe. One of the most detailed descriptions of Maio came from the pen of an unknown writer dubbed 'Hugo Falcandus', who wrote a chronicle of the court of King William I between 1154 and 1169. The author, referred to as the 'Psuedo-Falcandus' by modern historians—who also characterize his *History* as a "treacherous and often misleading source"—knew so many details of courtly life that he probably had some position in William's administration. This 'Falcandus' wasn't alone in disliking Maio, who was also hated by many nobles of south Italy. Falcandus pulls no punches: "And he [King William I] appointed as great admiral Maio of Bari, a man of humble origins who had first been a notary at court and then, step by step, reached the post of chancellor. This man was a beast such as whom no more repellent pest could be found, none more effective in achieving the destruction and overthrowing of the realm.... He had the ability to pretend and dissemble whatever he pleased; his mind, keen on sexual gratification, contrived intercourse with women married and unmarried, especially noble ones. He was particularly keen to overcome the chastity of those who had a reputation for decency."

Falcandus also accuses Maio of poisoning an archbishop and plotting to kill William to assume the crown for himself, but while Falcandus's account paints a monstrous portrait of Maio, other historical records indicate he was a pious man, and his building of San Cataldo, which served as the chapel to his house, was just one indication of his several acts of religious devotion. Maio became *Amir* at a rough time for Norman Sicily, during the much-contested reign of William I when the court was in particular disarray. Eventually, a rebel group recruited a young nobleman named Matthew Bonellus to assassinate Maio. Bonellus lay in wait on the evening of November 10th, 1160 and killed Maio with his sword in a shadowy alley near the Porta Santa Agata. The revolt came to a culmination when the palace was stormed and, according to Falcandus, the rebels raped the concubines, stole the money from the treasury, killed the court eunuchs, and imprisoned King William. William was soon saved, however, by the people of Palermo who still backed him. They gathered outside the palace demanding his release. The story was in every way a sad one. Not only was the king humiliated and the realm undermined, but the treasury was deprived of its wealth and the Christian citizens of Palermo, seizing the moment, killed many of the city's Muslims and looted their homes.

Further, William's son had imprudently peeked out a window during the storming of the palace and was killed by an arrow.

I thought that now would be the time to visit the Martorana and, sure enough, the last of the school groups was leaving. But as I approached the doorway there were three children on the porch, about seven or eight years old, with their names written on stickers on their shirts. One of them, Gabriella, explained that as a school project they were offering free tours of the Martorana and asked, in a tone that insisted on an affirmative, if I would like one. She pivoted with a whip of her brown pony tail and marched into the church, commanding me to follow. I obediently fell in line, not quite able to do anything else. She had her whole presentation memorized and delivered it breathlessly at a thousand words a minute, too fast for my middling Italian. She zipped me around her stations with an impressive assurance, authoritatively punctuating the completion of the circuit with a firm rap of her index finger on a sign-in book, instructing me to write my name, my country, and how good the tour was, which I certainly and happily did as she rushed off to acquire another client.

The church has a complex building history and changes began fairly soon after its construction. In 1588 the entrance was demolished and other parts were remodeled in virtually every subsequent century. The bell tower was built in the later middle ages and is pretty much unchanged from that time, though there used to be a dome on top of it. It's lost about ten feet of its original height. While originally Orthodox, the church served Catholics for more than seven centuries, but was returned to Orthodoxy after the Second World War to serve a refugee community of Albanian Orthodox Christians.

When Ibn Jubayr saw the Martorana in 1184 he thought it to be "one of the most wonderful constructions to be seen." Even today, more than eight centuries later, it's still breathtaking. The church has many names, such as the Church of the Admiral, the Church of Mary of the Admiral, *Santa Maria dell' Ammiraglio* in Italian, or simply the *Ammiraglio*. Sometimes it's even referred to as *San Nicolò dei Greci*, but its most common nickname is the Martorana, which might make you think it has something to do with Christian martyrs, but it gets this name from Eloise Martorana, the founding abbess of the Benedictine nunnery that used the church beginning in 1194. It was this group of nuns who began the practice of making colored marzipan in various shapes, a tradition that became an integral part of the holiday called *I Morti*, or 'The Dead', roughly equivalent to our Halloween, but taking place a couple of days later on November 2nd. In the older, more customary holiday children would write letters to their dead ancestors and ask for gifts, the parents would then hide the presents around the house for the kids to find. The day might also include a visit to the cemetery and the graves of earlier generations. The flower shops do a great business. Lately, *I Morti* has morphed into something more approximating Halloween in North America, but the tradition of the *Frutti di Martorana,* the colored marzipan creations, is still in full swing in Palermo and many bakeries and shops produce them. They're sometimes quite ambitious, such as sculptures of historical figures or complex trays of marzipan fruits or vegetables artfully tinted with food coloring to make them look realistic.

I took myself through the church at a more leisurely pace, while Gabriella raced a fashionably dressed German couple on the same *guida rapida* she'd given me. Their eyes were already glassing over. There are two marble columns in the church with Arabic inscriptions on them, verses from the Koran. If these columns could speak they'd have marvelous stories to tell. They likely began their careers as part of a Roman villa or small temple two thousand years ago, repurposed for a church when the Romans converted to Christianity in the 4th century CE, then purloined for a mosque when the Muslims conquered Sicily in the 9th century (receiving their inscriptions to purify them of any residual Christianity), and then reverting once more to Christian purposes when George built this chapel in 1140. These aren't the only Arabic inscriptions in the church. Around the base of the dome there's a narrow wooden band that also has Arabic writing in golden letters describing, of all things, the Greek Orthodox liturgy.

There are some stunning mosaics here, the most famous being the ones of the builder of the church, George of Antioch, prostrating himself before the Virgin Mary and the other of Christ crowning Roger II. In the first George, with flowing white hair and beard, kneels at the feet of Mary. From the hem of her robe, edged in gold, red tassels dangle. She lifts a delicate hand to affirm George's devotion, and holds a scroll with a Greek inscription: "O child [Christ], shield from all adversity George, the first of all archons who has built me this house from the foundations, and also all his family. Grant him absolution from his sins. For thou, O Word, as the only God, hast the power." Under this, another inscription, a caption for the one above, reads: "Petition of thy servant, George the Admiral." George looks as if he's emerging from a fancy red and gold sleeping bag, but it's his luxuriant robe curving over his back like a tortoise's shell. His arm looks stick-like and, oddly, becomes thicker towards his wrist, though that may be the fault of a poor restoration. In the upper right Christ pops out of a cloud and extends his hand towards Mary, indicating that George gets the thumbs-up. This mosaic and its inscriptions make more sense when you know that George's tomb, and the tomb of his wife, were once ensconced in front of this scene. In death, George hoped for salvation and a positive judgment of his life.

A mosaic in the opposite side of the church has a hovering Christ placing a crown on Roger II's head. An inscription in Greek letters above reads simply, Rogerios Rex: "Roger, King". Roger wears a bejeweled loros, an extravagant fashion accessory worn by the Byzantine emperors Roger wanted to emulate. It's a wide band that goes around his shoulders, waist and, finally, hangs from his left arm; the garment's fringe ornamented with teardrop pearls. Christ and Roger have serious frowns, indicating the momentousness of the event, as if that would make people believe that it actually happened. Neither of these two mosaics is in its original position, and they may have been damaged while being removed in one of the church's many renovations. At the bottom of the coronation scene the tesserae—the square bits a mosaic is made up of—are larger than those above and arranged in a disorderly fashion, indicating a seam between the original work and the sloppy repair job.

The church's original apse, alas, was demolished in 1680-85 and whatever medieval decorations that adorned it were destroyed. Now it's a baroque extravaganza upon which Benedictine nuns once gazed through upper rooms that flank the altar, witnessing the liturgies through the metal gratings that are still in place, and which blocked the congregation's view of the cloistered sisters. Over the church's entrance is an upper gallery for the women of the congregation, in Greek called a *gynaikonitis*.

In both Orthodox and medieval Catholic ceremonies men and women were kept apart, presumably to cut down on the girl-watching in church, which is too bad because the few times I went to church as a teenager I found looking at pretty girls a capital antidote for a tedious sermon. The only section that survives of the original building is the dome and a wide arch in front of it with two spectacular mosaics, one showing the *Nativity of Christ* and the other the *Koimesis* (the *Death of the Virgin*). In the *Nativity* the Virgin Mary, giant in scale compared to the other figures, sits on a white mattress in front of a cave. The ox and the ass peek into the cradle and seem delighted that their hay has been replaced by a baby. The ox smiles widely, like a character in a child's storybook. In the upper left an angel directs the shepherds' attention to the star, the elder of the two looking remarkably like George of Antioch. In the lower right the infant Christ appears again, here being bathed by midwives. One fills the basin while the other attentively tests the temperature of the water. In the lower left sits Joseph, his chin in his hand to indicate he was exhausted by the whole experience.

Opposite is the *Death of the Virgin*. Mary lies on her bier while St Peter swings a censer and St Paul mourns at her feet. St John tenderly places his head on her chest in a gesture of grief. The other apostles mourn, while Christ holds Mary's soul, represented as a swaddled baby. He raises her up, indicating he's taking her to heaven as angels fly down to receive her. To the right St Agnes, in a separate painted frame, seems to sadly contemplate the Virgin's departure.

The dramatic dome of the Martorana is occupied by a regal Pantocrator surrounded by a quartet of genuflecting archangels. Lower down is a ring of Old Testament prophets who point towards Christ, indicating he's the Messiah their visions foretold. They hold scrolls upon which those very prophesies are inscribed. The niches in the corners are inhabited by the four Evangelists—Matthew, Mark, Luke, and John—writing their gospels at wooden lecterns.

As Gabriella chalked up another tourist I snuck out into the sunlight again, my body anxious for a good walk.

Afternoon

I decided to go for a superfecta of medieval Norman churches and see the church of the Sicilian Vespers (Santo Spirito), which is in the cemetery grounds on the Via del Vespro south of the Porta Santa Agata, the only decently preserved medieval city gate from Palermo's old fortifications. It's on the Corso Tuköry, named after Luigi Tuköry, a Hungarian officer of Garibaldi's Expedition of the Thousand, who was killed in in 1860. His real name was Lajos Tuköry de Algyest. If you want to pay respects he's fashionably entombed in the church of San Domenico, where there are numerous exceptional nineteenth-century Neoclassical sepulchers. I walked by the medical university and hospital, with the cemetery right across the street, which I thought pessimistic but at the same time quite efficient. A silver Mercedes hearse cruised with funereal leisureliness by rows of flower shops, so I knew I was close. Still, I had to ask where the entrance was from one of the florists, who smiled and pointed his shears while holding a dripping bouquet of red roses.

The Palermo cemetery has thousands of tombs in every architectural style the city has ever known. There are Arab-Norman ones that look like mini versions of San Cataldo, there are Art Nouveau tombs, Gothic tombs, Classical and Neoclassical tombs, Renaissance-style tombs, even Fascist-style tombs. I really liked one of the Fascist mausoleums. I was ready to move in right away, picturing where I'd put the marble counter top and a Murphy bed. As I was exploring I saw the tomb of Giovanni Falcone, the judge who was killed by the mafia in 1992. It was, very rightly, in the Art Nouveau style in the spirit of Ernesto Basile: hopeful and elegant.

In the midst of the cemetery is Santo Spirito, built in the twelfth century by Archbishop William. It's also known as the Church of the Sicilian Vespers because of the incident at its doorstep on March 30th of 1282 that precipitated a violent revolt known as the Sicilian Vespers. On that fateful day a French soldier molested a Sicilian woman and a fight broke out, resulting in the soldier being killed by the woman's husband. That spark ignited an all-out revolution, the grievances of the Sicilian people against their foreign overlords erupting as violently as Mount Etna. The foreigners were identified by their inability to pronounce the word *ciceri* ('chickpeas') in the Sicilian dialect, and dispatched when they wavered. You should make note of this should your Italian enunciation be less than perfect. Legend has it that women suspected of carrying a Frenchman's child were put to the sword, their fetuses torn from their wombs, so deeply were the French despised.

The French nobleman Charles of Anjou had become king of Sicily and south Italy (the 'Kingdom of the Two Sicilies') in the complex political situation that emerged after the death of Frederick II. After Frederick's demise in 1250, his son Conrad ruled for four years and was succeeded by Manfred, who held power for a bit longer, until 1266. But the papacy had disliked Frederick and Germans in general. In 1261 a Frenchman, Jacques Pantaleon, was elected pope and took the name Urban IV, and he supported a French candidate who would be friendlier to the papacy than the Teutonic predecessors had been. This is how Sicily came under the rule of Charles and the French Angevins (i.e. from Anjou). Like so many of Sicily's occupiers the French taxed the natives of the island heavily and the life of the peasants was harsh. The inequalities and injustices led to the resentment that instigated the Vespers revolt. It is thought that on Easter Sunday of 1282 there were 2000 deaths in Palermo alone. The tragic events were immortalized in the 1855 opera by Verdi, *I Vespri Siciliani*.

I sat in the shade of a cypress tree, thinking of the tragedy that this spot evoked, one of so many Sicily has had to endure during its tumultuous history at the crossroads of empires. Nearby, an art student sat with her sketchbook, making a charcoal drawing of one of the tombs. With a gentle sweep along her cheek she restored to its place behind her ear a tendril of chestnut hair that a puff of wind had displaced. She bit her lip in concentration. Eight hundred years ago one of her forebears had been accosted by an arrogant Frenchman and Sicily had exploded in violence; possibly from the very spot where she now sat contemplatively outlining the curve of an arch. It made me think she was in Palermo at a great time, a time when the city was going to take its place once more among the Mediterranean's great cultural centers. I imagined her becoming an art restorer and preserving some of Palermo's great works for future generations.

A group of cemetery groundskeepers wearing fluorescent orange vests loitered near the entrance, smoking and chatting, posing like courting birds with bright plumage as they leaned on their rakes and watched co-eds from the university walk by. One clucked at a girl in a short skirt. I looked at my watch and realized I'd lingered a bit long. I had an appointment with Michele Anselmi, an expert on di Lampedusa's novel *The Leopard,* in an hour and a half. I walked quickly along the crowded spine of the Ballerò, dodging shoppers, and was back to the Casa Sicilia in time for a quick shower and a change of clothes.

Michele's apartment was nearby so it only took me five minutes to get there. I pressed his intercom button and he buzzed me up. He was on the third floor but I took the stairs, not completely trusting the elevator. There are some antique elevators in Palermo. If you're a history-of-elevators buff there are few places better. Myself, I've had some dodgy experiences. I like charming mechanical anachronisms as much as the next guy, but not when they strand me between floors. Michele was an old university chum of a friend of mine in Santa Cruz. He runs the *Parco Culturale del Gattopardo,* a literary group dedicated to the study of Giuseppe di Lampedusa and his great novel *The Leopard.* He organizes tours where he takes people around to all the places mentioned in the novel. He has walks like 'Palermo Through the Eyes of Giuseppe di Lampedusa' and 'A Walk with the Leopard'. Some of them go beyond Palermo to places such as Santa Margherita di Belice, the town that Donnafugata was based on in the novel. Michele greeted me with a broad smile and we went to his living room and we talked about *The Leopard* and what an incomparable window onto history it was, worth more than a hundred academic books on the history of mid-nineteenth-century Palermo.

The novel's main character is Don Fabrizio, the Prince of Salina, an aristocrat whose social class is in eclipse; he represents the last vestiges of feudalism in Sicily. The story is set in 1860, the year when Garibaldi's troops—the 'Garibaldini', his famous red-shirted Expedition of the Thousand—were liberating Sicily from Bourbon rule and attempting to unify the island with the emerging state of Italy, a crucial stage in the longer historical process known as the *Risorgimento* ('Resurgence', ca. 1815-1871), which eventually led to the formation of the Italian nation. By this time the Sicilian nobility was virtually dissolute. The Bourbon regime had already begun to undermine their power by instituting agrarian reforms and trying to turn land over to peasants in the hope that they would be more responsible, more productive, and less restless.[19] Many nobles sold their properties and estates to raise cash to maintain their profligate lifestyles. A British traveler, John Galt, visited Sicily in the first decade of the nineteenth century and saw that this dramatic process had already begun. He gives an account of a decrepit baron outside his crumbling house trying to sell his watch, crying as he gestured towards his once grand home, "This is my palace, but I have nothing to eat!" In the Palermo of those decades one could find a pawnbroker's shop on virtually every corner, their overflowing shelves barometers of the aristocracy's decline as they deaccessioned their belongings. The Reverend Thomas S. Hughes, another Briton, visited the island 1812 and had sober remarks about the nobles of Palermo. While he observed the grandeur of their lifestyle he noted that, "...this splendor was chiefly external, for the prime comforts of domestic life, as well as the pleasures of refined taste and rational society, were lamentably sacrificed to vain parade and ostentatious decoration: ambitious poverty was preferred to elegant economy, and the appearance of happiness to its reality. Thus, though the public promenade of the Marina glittered every evening with its elegant equipages and gaudy liveries, many noble mansions exhibited most disgusting scenes of penury and meanness."

In Lampedusa's novel Don Fabrizio attempts to hold on to his dignity amidst his estate's decline. Around him the structures of the centuries-old feudal hierarchy dissolve just as the nobles' palaces crumble. The Prince, too, is old. He will die at story's end. Modernity destabilizes the medieval order of things, atop which he and his forebears have stood, and he is powerless to stop it, aware he belongs "to an unfortunate generation, swung between the old world and the new." New hierarchies emerge, with men who know how to capitalize on the changing of the guard and the opportunities for power and position it brings. His beloved nephew, Tancredi, warns his uncle, "If we want things to stay as they are, things will have to change."

Michele knew the novel line by line and I'd just read it again and had it more or less at my fingertips, so we had a great time talking about the book's characters and the portrait it presents of a key moment in Sicily's history. Michele brought up the minor character of Russo, one of the Prince's dependents, who is a low-grade but ambitious mafioso: "Clever, dressed rather smartly in a striped velvet jacket, with greedy eyes below a remorseless forehead, the Prince found in him a perfect specimen of a class on its way up." Garibaldi's armies have arrived in Sicily and mafiosi such as Russo have thrown their support behind him. Russo has stolen hundreds of baskets of lemons from Don Fabrizio, which may seem a petty theft, but it's likely he's stealing other things as well, supplementing his income at the expense of his patron whose own fortunes are rapidly dwindling. From these profits Russo lends money as a loan shark and buys land cheap from desperate owners. He is the prince's estate manager, but also has dealings on the side. Many in his position did the same during these years and they came to exploit the peasant farmers as ruthlessly as the nobles had done in earlier centuries. Russo implies things will be fine, as if he already knows how things will play out, and promises the Prince and his estate protection. In fact, he will not protect the Prince, unless he makes it worth his while, rather, he will situate himself to profit from the Prince's social and financial demise.

Later we meet Russo's foil, the devoted steward of Donnafugata, Don Onofrio Rotolo, "who was one of the rare persons held in esteem by the Prince, and perhaps the only one who had never cheated him". His honesty, Lampedusa writes, "was on the verge of mania, and spectacular tales were told of it." Don Onofrio keeps to the medieval model of fealty and unquestioning devotion to his lord. Michele offered me coffee, which at the time I sorely needed, and mentioned Lampedusa's description of another of the new opportunists, Don Calogero Sedàra, the mayor of Donnafugata, who had become rich buying up properties from cash-strapped nobles: "Then came the private news… [of] the rapid rise to fortune of Don Calogero Sedàra; six months ago a mortgage arranged by the latter with Baron Tumio had been foreclosed, and he had gained possession of the estate; thus by the loan of a thousand ounces of gold he now owned a property which yielded five hundred ounces a year … he had also made some very profitable sales of grain in the period of confusion and famine after the [Garibaldi's] landings."

Michele told me a telling statistic that reflected the trend in the decades before 1860: in 1812 there were 2000 owners of land, by 1860 there were 20,000. The Bourbon regime had moved to curb the power of the nobles through land distribution to the peasantry, thus the great estates of the nobles were already being fragmented and redistributed by the time Garibaldi landed his forces at Marsala. But the land, while going to more men, and to new men, still left tens of thousands of peasants landless and powerless. To give an idea of the moral compasses of these new men, Lampedusa adds, almost as an afterthought, that Sedàra has made profits by speculating on grain and overcharging the starving poor for food during the confusion created by Garibaldi's landing. Later in the story it's also suggested that he murdered his troublesome father-in-law and, as mayor of Donnafugata, rigged recent elections in his favor. Even in the late twentieth century the mafia could deliver the Sicilian vote to the Christian Democratic Party of Italy, thereby earning favors from federal representatives in Rome.

The Sedàras and their ilk were smart enough to support Garibaldi, so that when he was victorious they were rewarded with public positions—all the Bourbon bureaucrats having been driven from their offices—thus taking advantage of the social and political conflicts to insinuate themselves into both the new economy and new state, adding political power to the financial power they had already obtained. Michele related these new men to the *capi* or 'heads' of mafia clans. Thus a new rapacious criminal / capitalist class replaced the older noble class, the former no less exploitive of the peasantry than the latter. When the Prince of Salina's nephew, Tancredi, tells his uncle that he is going to join Garibaldi the Prince responds, "You're mad, boy, to go with those people! They're all in the *maffia,* all troublemakers."

The novel's events take place in that fateful May of 1860. Five years later, the word '*maffia*' first appears in official documents of the Prefect of Palermo, Count Gualterio, who noted they were a criminal group "growing in audacity." The word 'mafia' did not always have negative connotations. One of the early meanings of the word in Palermo slang, used well into the last century, implied 'stylish', 'manly', and 'respected'. Michele told me that when he was a teenager and bought a new hat or other clothes that made him look good his aunt would flatter him, saying *"che mafioso!"*

Lampedusa was himself of the nobility, among the last of his line, the Tomasi di Lampedusa. The title of the book was derived from his family coat of arms, which sports a rampant leopard, and it was partly on the accounts of his great grandfather, Giulio Fabrizio, that Lampedusa was drawing when he wrote his masterpiece.[20] In photographs the late-blooming author, who took up writing seriously only in his fifties, looks as exhausted as his class, with sunken, weary eyes. Even in a picture taken at the age of two he seems listless. He wears a frilly frock and stands on an ornate chair with elaborate wainscoting behind him and a decorative Chinese vase on a baroque table to the right; a study in excessive ornament, as if embodying the superfluity of the class he'd been born into. Lampedusa didn't live to see his novel published, receiving rejections even as he fought lung cancer in his last months. Not long after his death on July 23 1957, an acceptance letter finally came and the novel was published in November of 1958. The next year it was awarded the Strega prize, the highest honor in Italian fiction. By 1960 it had gone through over fifty editions and was considered to be one of the greatest Italian novels ever written.

I left Michele's apartment at dusk. I'd never considered how many characters in *The Leopard* prefigured the mafia, so I'd found Michele's observations fascinating, even more so as tomorrow as I had an appointment to meet Umberto Santino, one of the world's foremost experts on the mafia and on the history of the anti-mafia movement.

☙

DAY SEVEN

He who is silent and bows his head dies every time he does so. He who speaks aloud and walks with his head held high dies only once.

-Giovanni Falcone

The fight against the mafia… must be not only a cold and repressive struggle, but a moral and cultural movement, involving everyone, especially younger generations, the most apt to feel the beauty of the renewed taste of freedom.

-Paolo Borsalino, from a speech at Giovanni Falcone's funeral

You did not kill them.
Their ideas walk on our legs.

-Protest banners after the murders of Falcone & Borsellino

The long walk to Umberto's place was made pleasant by an ascending sun dissipating the misty clouds that had wearily settled in the geological bowl of Palermo during the cool of the night. The sun, a magnesium white through the persisting veils, set its thinning adversaries swirling, assisted by a fresh breeze tumbling off the slopes of

Monte Pellegrino. I arrived in his neighborhood quite early so I stopped at a sidewalk café and enjoyed some coffee and a *treccina* (literally, a 'pigtail'; a braided pastry) while I watched people rush to work, like all Italians, in the best shoes you've ever seen in your life.

Umberto Santino is a major figure in the anti-mafia movement and a respected historian of the mafia. He's spent most of his life educating the public and being an activist for civil society and human rights. As I approached his building I found it ironic that the apartment of an anti-mafia crusader would be in one of the very concrete high rises that the mafia built in the 1960s in the Sack of Palermo, as the era of the destruction of historical buildings and the erection of substandard concrete high-rises is sometimes called. Umberto greeted me and when I entered I was a bit taken aback. I thought I was visiting him in his apartment, but instead of a couch and television I saw a library and archive. In what would have been the dining room was a study table. Files reached to the ceiling and books lined every wall. Document boxes were squirreled away in every conceivable niche, and yet it was all perfectly ordered. I got the feeling that if I had a specific document in mind Umberto could find it within five seconds. These were the offices of the organization Umberto and his wife Anna Puglisi founded in 1977, the *Centro Siciliano di Documentazione Giuseppe Impastato.*

The center is named after Giuseppe Impastato (nicknamed Peppino) a young man who was born in 1948 into a mafia family in the town of Cinisi just north of Palermo, where the airport is today (lord knows who lies beneath the concrete of those runways). This isn't an incidental location. The mafia historian John Dickie notes how the airport was a crucial transport hub for contraband. Of the 8000 inhabitants of Cinisi, about 6400 of them had relatives in the U.S., a large percentage of them in Detroit. Peppino's father and uncle were both mafiosi and in 1963 the uncle, Cesare Manzella, the mafia boss of Cinisi, was murdered with a car bomb. Peppino, only fifteen years old, was so shocked by his relative's violent death that he became an energetic anti-mafia crusader. Eventually, Peppino started a radio show and organized consciousness-raising activities in his community. He had a biting sense of humor and brazenly mocked the culture of the mafia, despite the fact that his family was still involved in the organization and pleaded with him to desist. It was when Peppino tried to gain real political influence by running in the Cinisi council elections that the mafia finally intervened. On the evening of May 9th, 1978 he was tied to train tracks and a bomb detonated under his body. Astonishingly, corrupt (or terrified) police detectives tried to classify it as a suicide. On the same day in Rome, in a slaying that received significantly more world attention, the Christian Democrat Aldo Moro, the former Prime Minister of Italy, was murdered by the Marxist Red Brigade terrorists who had kidnapped him weeks before. This more headline-grabbing assassination relegated Peppino's death to the back pages. In the backlash against the mafia Peppino was posthumously elected to the Cinisi town council and his example inspired many to take up the anti-mafia cause, including Santino.[21]

Umberto told me of the continuing challenges of fighting corruption and mafia activities in Palermo and Sicily in general. "The mafia of old is gone, in a way", he said, "but its structures not only survive but have now been adapted to more 'legitimate' modern institutions. The problem is", Santino told me, "that it's hard to tell the legal money from the illegal money", so seamlessly are criminal activities merged with legitimate ones; the money circulating in the complex system of international banking and finance. Drugs are still an important part of the economics of mafia profits, but prostitution and human trafficking are also important. "It's a myth, this idea that the mafia don't do that, that they don't dirty themselves with prostitution. We are looking into the appearance of African girls here in Palermo." I thought of the girls I'd seen in the woods on the way to Mondello. As Umberto talked it made me wonder how he must have negotiated his life in Palermo all these years, to be so energetic as an activist and productive as a scholar and yet still, well… and yet still be alive. I asked him if he ever feared for his life, but he dodged the question. Maybe it was a stupid one. Or maybe his silence on the subject provided an eloquent answer.

It's hard to know when and where the mafia began, though most historians trace its roots to around 1860 at the time that Garibaldi invaded. But mafia-like groups or criminal brotherhoods seem to have existed well before this time. The English traveler George Sandys made a visit to Sicily as part of his grand tour of the Eastern Mediterranean in 1610, and he noted that the interior of the island was dangerous. He wrote that "the uplands inhabitants are so inhospitable to strangers, that between them both there is no travelling by land without a strong guard; whom rob and murder whomever they can conveniently lay hold of."

When Patrick Brydone travelled through Sicily in the spring of 1770, a gentleman told him of a particular group of bandits: "He says that in some circumstances these bandits (*banditti*) are the most respectable people on the island; and have by much the highest and most romantic notions of what they call their point of honour. That, however criminal they may be with regard to society in general, yet, with respect to one another, and to every person to whom they have once professed it, they have ever maintained the most unshakable fidelity. The magistrates have often been obliged to protect them, and even pay them court, as they are known to be perfectly determined, and desperate; and so extremely vindictive, that they will certainly put any person to death, who has ever given them just cause of provocation." It would be difficult to come up with a more succinct, if partial, definition of the mafia—the corruption of the judiciary and what later came to be known as *aggiustare processi* ('adjusting trials'), and the threat of assassination to those who provoke them; even, presumably, judges who defy them. Their violence is balanced by their *omertà*, their total devotion to each other and their code of honor, a moral chiasmus reflected in the story of a mafiosi stabbed by another mafiosi, who, with his last breath told his murderer, "If I live I'll kill you, if I die I'll forgive you."

The valleys south of Palermo towards cities such as Trapani and Castelveltrano were particularly dangerous and became known as 'the bandits' corridor'. Brydone passed through this area on his way to Palermo and just outside the walls he saw the city administration's response: "Near the city we passed a place of execution, where the quarters of a number of robbers were hung up upon hooks, like so many hams; some of them appeared recently executed and made a very unsightly figure." Dismemberment and hanging wasn't the only form of capital punishment in eighteenth-century Palermo. Joseph Hager saw a beheading in 1796: "At Palermo, decapitation is performed by means of a machine, similar to the guillotine, called a *Manara*. I saw the lawyer Blasi beheaded by it; being convicted of a desire to effect a revolution in Sicily."

Yet while the cities may have been better

policed, the peripheries remained lawless frontiers. The countryside of Sicily was dangerous from the Middle Ages right through to the twentieth century. In the sixteenth century an official knew of armed groups who "prevented farmers leaving their houses to work the land...We hear of nothing but killings, kidnappings, the theft of cattle, farmsteads burnt and women raped." Hager also observed that "the country has long been infested with armed *banditti,* who in parties, amounting to some hundreds, have frequently committed the most daring depredations. They are provided with firearms; and they have not only been known to plunder the unprotected traveler, but also to commit the most atrocious murders." Well into the late nineteenth century the situation remained unchanged. When Leopoldo Francetti went to Sicily in 1876 to prepare a report on the island's political and administrative circumstances he heard many tales of the violence in the countryside just beyond the confines of Palermo's walls. Of the bucolic orchards of the verdant Conca d'Oro, after hearing stories of brutal murders, he wrote, "After a certain number of these stories the scents of orange and lemon blossoms begin to seem like [the stench of] corpses." Sicilians seemed to have got a kick out of frightening foreigners with tales of murder and violence. In *The Leopard,* there's a scene where Tancredi is taking a visitor to Sicily around Donnafugata, and he is "assailed," Lampedusa writes, "by the singular island itch to tell foreigners tales that were revolting but unfortunately quite true."

The tale of the countryside around Palermo is a long story, centuries old, of poverty and exploitation. The specific historical and social circumstances that gave rise to the mafia in western Sicily after the chaos before, during, and after Garibaldi's military operations of 1860-61, as well as the fracturing of the economic power of the nobility and the brutal Bourbon regime that, nonetheless, failed to bring order to the countryside, provided perfect nourishment for the development of an organized criminal class that had already institutionalized itself centuries before in the shadow economies and fraternities of the ungoverned interior hill towns and country byways. The mafiosi helped Garibaldi and Garibaldi helped the mafiosi, and when he departed, soon to be wounded and captured in the Battle of Aspromonte, the mafia *capi* (heads), many derived from the managers of the noble estates, easily occupied the vacuum of power left by the absence of authority exercised by either the state or the now obsolete nobility.

Strangely, this chronicle became interwoven with American history. In the 1880s, when American grain production and exports undercut Sicilian agricultural markets, the island became even more impoverished, instigating mass emigration to America, bringing not only hard working citizens but those, too, who brought with them mafia culture and connections that in later years would have dramatic ramifications for American crime. Beginning in the 1890s Sicilians emigrated at a rate of about 150,000 a year until 1913, the vast majority of them to the United States. It was in these years that the Sicilian mafia established a foothold in America, providing a foundation for future growth and collaboration with their brethren in Sicily. But grain wasn't the only commodity that had a mafia connection. Dickie tells the story of the mafia's origins in the lemon groves of the area around Palermo.[22] Remember in *The Leopard* the estate manager (*sovrastante*, or 'overseer') Russo steals crates of lemons from Don Fabrizio. This is no randomly chosen commodity, as lemons and oranges were hugely valuable exports at the time. As Dickie points out, the British navy bought lemons for its sailors, to avert scurvy, and used the oil of the bergamot, another citrus fruit, to flavor Earl Grey tea. America was also hungry for lemons: "In 1834, over 400,000 cases of lemons were exported. By 1850 it was 750,000. In the mid-1880s an astonishing 2.5 million cases of Italian citrus fruit arrived in New York every year, most of them from Palermo. In 1860, the year of Garibaldi's expedition, it was calculated that Sicily's lemon groves were the most profitable agricultural land in Europe."

Lemon trees really did turn the Conca d'Oro into gold, but the success of the crops was dependent on many factors, such as irrigation, and they were easily vandalized, thus making the withholding of water or the threat of destruction an easy path to ill-gotten gains. Early mafia *cosche* (families) specialized in extortion or providing protection for the groves and the safe transportation of the produce to the port for shipping. Those who didn't pay would find their orchards starved for water or destroyed, or their shipments high-jacked on the road to Palermo, or, in extreme cases, their honest managers killed, then the owners forced to hire a corrupt mafioso as a replacement, lest they or a family member suffer a similar fate.[23]

While the mafia may have developed early on in the former agricultural estates of the nobility and the bucolic but deadly groves of the Conca d'Oro, the countryside just beyond was also filled with opportunities for exploitation. Donkeys could be stolen, or cattle rustled and brought to mafia-controlled butchers in Palermo. Sheep and goats, too, were surreptitiously rounded up by armed gangs and smuggled through the city gates and sold on the black markets that thrived in Palermo's labyrinthine alleyways and unregulated fruit, vegetable, and meat markets, just as illegal Bluefin tuna appear in them today. All manner of produce were likewise vulnerable to the dark market in goods and services the mafia imposed on ordinary people.

The mafia of the countryside prospered and had their people in Palermo as well, a city mafia that was their urban counterpart and complement. These two realms, country and city, and the *cosche* who ran these jurisdictions, coexisted in relative balance for decades, even during the Fascist period, when mafiosi were united in their resistance to the government's determined efforts to extirpate them from the island, an effort led by Cesare Mori, Mussolini's 'Iron Prefect of Palermo', whose methods were often just as violent as the mafia's.

Like the devil, the most ingenious thing the mafia ever did was convince people it didn't exist. Through history, Palermo's streets were very often safe, though occasional battles would erupt between mafia families for territory. It reminds me of the time I went to Las Vegas and took a taxi from the airport. The driver was very old and I asked him how long he'd been driving and he said, "since 1962". I commented that he must have seen many changes and he replied that Las Vegas was terrible today, that he liked it much better when the mafia was in charge of everything. Surprised, I asked him why, and he said "Because there wasn't any crime." Well into the twentieth century there were many people, including Sicilians, who didn't think the mafia was real, that it was an invention of foreigners and northern Italians who wanted to insult Sicilians and paint a picture of them as brutal and backward. This is why, unless a specific statement was supposed to be made by a murder, the mafia preferred the *"lupara bianca"*, the "white shotgun", assassination, that is, a murder for which no body is ever found, thus leaving it open as to whether one ever actually took place.[24] People would simply disappear, leaving only rumor behind.

There's a story that may or may not be true, or, most likely, may be partly true. It's been claimed that when the Allies were planning the invasion of Sicily during World War II the American military contacted the New York mobster Lucky Luciano and made a deal with him, so that when General Patton and the Americans landed in Sicily for Operation Husky on July 9th of 1943 they moved almost without resistance to Palermo because Luciano had united the mafiosi of western Sicily to run the Fascists out just ahead of the invasion. Patton was welcomed in Palermo as a liberator, even though Allied planes had just bombed the city's port and historic core to oblivion. Of course, just as with Garibaldi, when the Americans left they had to reward those who had helped them and the mafia became as powerful as it had ever been as corrupt officials filled the power vacuum left behind by the defeated Fascists. Resolutely anti-communist, because exploitation of the impoverished Sicilian peasantry was an important part of their organization, and fervently anti-Fascist, the mafia flourished during the Cold War as the brutal but useful shadow power in Sicily, which lived securely in the shade of the centrist Christian Democratic Party of Italy. The Sicilian mafia delivered the goods to the politicians—votes—and the politicians delivered protection from prosecution and government largesse for projects the mafia could exploit.

In the mid-1950s through the 1970s there

gradually developed an imbalance between the urban and the rural mafia. It began when vast sums of money from Rome were directed to Sicily, and most specifically to Palermo, for public housing projects. The city mafia entered the construction business. Many of the nineteenth-century villas of the *Nuova Citta* along the spine of the Via della Libertà were demolished and shoddy high rise apartments were thrown up in their places. The extensive gardens of the old villas were bulldozed and ever more apartments packed cheek to jowl, leaving few open spaces for the new tenants, who were vacating—perhaps understandably—the slum-like warrens of the old city in droves for the modern apartments. When Piersanti Mattarella, the president of the Sicilian regional government, passed a law in 1980 requiring buildings to be constructed to a safety code consistent with the rest of Italy, the mafia murdered him. Today, you're more likely to be killed by concrete falling off one of these substandard, deteriorating buildings than by an act of violent crime. Even the terrible Belice Earthquake in January of 1968, which killed hundreds of people in western Sicily, couldn't make people adopt more stringent standards of construction. Parts of the lovely Conca d'Oro, too, had their idyllic orchards razed and apartment blocks hastily assembled over the remains, turning parts of that verdant green belt into a cement suburb.

The Palermo mafia families made extraordinary profits in those years, revenues that the mafia families of the countryside didn't partake of in equal measure. The imbalance became even more pronounced when American and European authorities broke up what was known as 'The French Connection' where labs in Marseille were processing Middle Eastern opium into heroin. After the bust, many of those labs were relocated to Palermo, and as the popularity of the drug skyrocketed in America, encouraged by the marketing and distribution of the American mafia families, the Palermo bosses made astronomical amounts of money, thereby increasing both their social respectability and political power. The mafia *cosche* of the rural peripheries felt the traditional equity between the countryside and the city hadn't been respected. Further, as the Palermitan mafiosi became richer, they tended to see their now poorer county cousins as hicks, at times referring to them as *viddani* or 'peasants'.

This sense that they were disrespected by their urban counterparts, as well as the imbalance in profits, led to the first mafia war, which was led by the mafia family from Corleone, a small mountain village 56 kilometers (35 miles) south as the bullet flies from Palermo. There were many mafia wars, their tragedies providing some of the historical material for Mario Puzo's 1969 novel *The Godfather* and Francis Ford Coppola's cinematic adaptation, which centered on a fictional American mafia *cosche* that traced its name and ancestry to Corleone. The years from around 1960 through the 1980s were terrible years for Sicily and Italy in general, with competing ideologies from the right and left intermingled with the mafia in power struggles. These decades were so violent they are called the *anni di piombo* ('years of lead') because of the number of shootings, to say nothing of the bombings and other methods of murder.[25] The early eighties, in particular, are sometimes called the *mattanza*, evoking the slaughter of the tuna.

A central figure of this tragedy was the vicious mafia boss of Corleone, Salvatore Riina, nicknamed *La Belva* ('The Beast'). Riina had inherited the positon from the earlier Corleone boss Luciano Leggio, also well known for his ruthlessness. Riina hit the Palermo mafia *cosche* hard, even having other mafia *capi* such as Stefano Bontade and Salvatore Inzerillo murdered in 1981. Riina raised money through kidnappings without obtaining permission from the mafia commission or *cupola*, the governing group of the mafia families. Earlier mafia kidnappings (though this was not by the Sicilian mafia) had included, in 1973, the famous abduction of Eugene Getty, the grandson of John Paul Getty, netting a ransom of 2.5 million dollars, which the penurious grandfather grudgingly paid—calling it a loan to his grandson, which he presumably had to pay back—after Eugene's ear appeared in a mail parcel. In time Riina acquired sufficient resources to get into the heroin processing and exporting business himself, which eventually led to the Corleonese becoming the most powerful entity in the Sicilian mafia. By the end of the 1970s the Corleonese had major processing labs in Mazara del Vallo and Alcamo. Between 1978 and 1980 four to five tons of heroin worth six hundred million US dollars in annual profits were produced in Sicily.

By the late 1980s and early 1990s Giovanni Falcone had become the mafia's worst enemy. From the *pentito* ('penitent', 'confessor' or 'informant'; a mafiosi who provides evidence to prosecutors) Tommaso Buscetta's testimonies, Falcone had learned much about the complex culture of the mafia. Falcone's experience in forensic accounting had given him investigative tools to follow the money in ways that earlier prosecutors had been unable to do. Further, Falcone and Borsellino had nurtured international cooperation with European and American law enforcement to get a sense of the multinational web of mafia connections.

It was Riina who had the prosecutors Giovanni Falcone and Paolo Borsellino killed. At around 6:00 pm on May 23rd of 1992 Falcone, along with his wife (Francesca Morvillo, also a judge) driver, and police escort were all killed with a thousand-pound bomb placed in a conduit—by the use of a skateboard—under the Capaci exit of the main highways from the airport to Palermo. The Capaci Massacre, as it came to be known, was shocking even in a city used to mafia assassinations. Less than two months later, on July 19th, Falcone's friend and partner in mafia investigations and prosecutions, Paolo Borsellino, was killed by a car bomb in the street in front of his mother's home. Even though a warrant had been issued for his arrest, Riina was not apprehended until a decade after the assassinations, because law enforcement authorities were 'unable to find him'. And yet Riina had, for the entire time, been living openly in Palermo under his real name.

The most compelling images of these terrible decades are found in the incomparable photographs of Letizia Battaglia, a photographer and journalist who courageously confronted the mafia with her unapologetic photographic documentation of assassinations. Not all of her photography was morose; she also lovingly recorded many happier images of the people and life of Palermo. Shooting with high contrast black and white film, her images are haunting and journalistic in their directness, while also at times poetic and even surrealistic. Her hundreds of thousands of images she would darkly refer to as her "archive of blood." She worked for years for the newspaper *L'Ora*, a left wing paper which was a thorn in the side of the mafia. The mafia bombed its offices in 1958 after it ran a damning report on the Corleonese *capo* Luciano Leggio, and murdered the *L'Ora* journalist Mauro de Mauro in 1970 for his exposés. Battaglia wasn't just a photographer and a journalist. She also ran for political office and was a city council member with the Green Party from 1985 to 1991. Later, she became a member of the regional parliament from 1991 to 1996 as a representative of *La Rete* ('The Nework') a party founded by Palermo's anti-mafia mayor Leoluca Orlando, with whom Battaglia also worked to preserve the historical architecture of the old city, helping to begin what has come to be known as the *Primavera di Palermo,* the 'Palermo Spring'; a hopeful season that thankfully continues.

The murders of the much admired crusaders Falcone and Borsellino led to a virulent backlash against the mafia, a reaction which, though not fatal, has in the intervening decades diminished the mafia's stranglehold on Palermo. Part of the reaction in the 1990s took a novel form known as the *comitato dei lenzuoli bianchi* or 'Committee of the White Sheets', where citizens displayed their anti-mafia sentiments with white sheets or table cloths hung from their balconies, sometimes with slogans painted on them. Battaglia notes that in some areas, where older housewives were still afraid of the mafia, they wouldn't hang out a sheet, but would come to their balconies and discretely shake a tablecloth as the protesters marched by.

There's a Moreton Bay Fig on the sidewalk at Via Emanuele Notarbartolo, 23 called the *Albero di Falcone* or 'Falcone Tree'. It's outside what used to be Giovanni Falcone's home. Since 1992, every year on May 23rd, the citizens of Palermo gather around the tree to remember Falcone and Borsellino and their courageous fight against crime and corruption.

Thousands attend the ceremonies and the continued commitment against mafia activities. For me it's Palermo's most evocative and touching anti-mafia monument, partly because of its location on the Via Emanuele Notarboltolo. Notarbotolo was the first of all the *cadaveri eccellenti* or 'illustrious corpses', a term given to those honest public officials who were killed for fighting the mafia or who were so honest as to be above corruption, thus threatening mafia ambitions. Notarbartolo was stabbed to death in a railway car in 1893, a century before Falcone was killed, giving a profound historical context for the city's long fight against *Cosa Nostra,* "Our Thing", as these criminals came to call their vicious brotherhood. As I walked up the street I could see it easily. It's quite a big tree, and the Moreton Bay Fig can become enormous, so one wonders what will give way as the tree is already crowding out an apartment building. Most agree that it will have to be the apartment that goes. The tree was completely covered in papers, folders, even t-shirts with anti-mafia slogans. You couldn't see the trunk. People left myriad votive offerings, as if it was a religious shrine. Some had written their comments on paper and put them in plastic sleeves so they wouldn't spoil in the rain. I wrote my own letter to Falcone and tucked it into one of the folders that had several notes inside. I wondered if someone came and collected these things and archived them, as they've done with many of the September 11th materials left at Ground

Zero. I checked my spelling, just in case. A couple of guys eyed me, but mostly people just walked by, finding nothing strange in a tourist leaving a letter to a tree. I waited for a while, wondering if another pilgrim would show up, a fellow believer who I could commune with, maybe go have coffee with and talk about Falcone, but I suppose this isn't really a tourist spot. There was no tree priest to hear my confession or prayer. Life went on along the busy street.

Another powerful anti-mafia monument, unfortunately situated, is the fifty-foot steel tower erected in the busy roundabout at the Piazza XIII Vittime (Piazza of the Thirteen Victims) just north of the old port. Designed by the sculptor Mario Pecoraino, it was put up in 1983 in memory of Pio La Torre and Carlo Alberto Dalla Chiesa who were murdered in 1982,[26] but its inscription, which reads *ai caduti lotta contra la mafia* ("to the fallen in the struggle against the mafia") is more inclusive, memorializing all who have been killed in the anti-mafia movement. Constructed by the engineers of the Palermo naval shipyards, of durable anti-corrosive steel, it's unapologetically phallic, but also indicates the resolve of the anti-mafia crusaders. It's odd to see a modernist, abstract sculpture in Palermo, but I suppose the artist thought that the abstraction reflected the modernity of the struggle. I like it, but its location isn't amenable to the contemplation its subject evokes. A high hedge around the park would dramatically improve the space by isolating it from the continual flow of noisy traffic that streams around it. There's a symbolic reason for the location, however, as the piazza was already named after victims of oppression and violence, hence Piazza of the Thirteen Victims, and there was already a small obelisk to those fatalities twenty-five meters south of the tower. The thirteen were victims of a Bourbon crackdown in 1860 in the town of Gancia, a massacre that did much to sway Sicilian opinion against Bourbon rule at a key moment on the eve of Garibaldi's invasion.[27] With the placement of the anti-mafia monument in this same piazza, the fight against the mafia was equated with the domination of foreign regimes, and thus, in a way, became paralleled with the struggle for Sicilian freedom from oppressors both foreign and domestic.

When I left Umberto's I took a bus to the old town and walked in the meandering alleys east of the Carmelite church. This is and always will be my favorite Palermo. I anticipate with some sadness its gentrification, a process that has already begun. As I was walking home I passed by a small derelict square in which a boy, about seven years old, was indifferently kicking an underinflated soccer ball against a wall beside a garbage bin. He saw me and snatched up the worn ball and stared with eyes wide open, as if I was a giraffe. He wore a tattered gray sweater with holes at the elbows. I smiled and gave a little wave as he pivoted slowly, keeping me in his sights. Only later that night, as I was falling asleep, did I realize that maybe he wasn't looking at me because I was a rare bird of a tourist in his neighborhood, but because he just wanted someone to play with. I'll always regret not taking ten minutes to kick that threadbare ball around his forsaken piazza and help him turn it into a cheering stadium where he scored the winning goal for Italy in the World Cup final.

☙

DEPARTURE

The entrance to Palermo is very striking...from the beautiful amphitheater of mountains which form the bay; and more especially that of Santa Rosalia, generally called Monte Pellegrino, from the hermitage on its summit; which rises directly from the harbor...

-Arthur John Strutt, 1842

This final morning I planned to make my pilgrimage to Santa Rosalia's cavern on Monte Pellegrino, the city's most revered religious shrine. I woke up at 7:00, had a hot shower—for once getting in there before my fellow inmates at the Casa Sicilia exhausted the hot water tank—had some cereal and tea for breakfast, and left by a respectable 8:30. I walked to the Piazza Ruggiero Settimo, bought a couple of bus tickets at the Ribaudo Tabacci kiosk, and waited for the 812 bus at the stop just north of the Teatro Politeama. The morning light was doing some interesting things with the statues on the theater, so I pulled out my telephoto lens and tried to catch the effects. A lady at the stop looked at me and smiled, pointed at the statue and said, *"molto artistico!"* The bus arrived in about fifteen minutes with only three people on it. It was a great tour of the town, going up past the Ucciardone prison and finally beginning the ascent of the mountain along its winding switchbacks. The driver took the corners like a Formula One contestant, almost killing a family of four in a yellow Fiat Cinquecento, but taking it all in stride. Even the family was nonplussed and smiling cheerily as we passed. Apparently it was only I who required a change of underwear.

The higher we got the more dramatic the views of Palermo became. I caught fleeting glimpses through blurry pines of the city awash in morning light. In the port cranes loomed, looking much like the birds they're named after. I imagined one leaning down and snatching up a stevedore with its beak. A big ferry boat was in, the one from Naples, and a cruise ship beyond it. The bus took us looping dizzily around the mountain, finally braking with a shudder at the foot of the windswept staircase leading to Santa Rosalia's grotto, where a few souvenir shops and cafes were sleepily assembled. Some proprietors were sluggishly arranging their wares; others slouched pessimistically under their shelters, keeping an eye on the somber clouds restless winds were pushing over the mountain. Perhaps, gazing heavenwards, they were praying for a caravan of buses containing Polish Catholics eager for pious knickknacks.

The staircase isn't very long and more zealous devotees go up on their knees to make it more challenging and masochistic, but I bounded up with a merry atheism. I figured the bed at the Casa Sicilia was providing sufficient penitence. A baroque façade was constructed in front of the cave, making the ensemble look more church-like and creating an interior forecourt to increase the capacity of the site. It was so peaceful, with only me and four other people, that I found it difficult to imagine how overwhelmed this place must be around the time of Rosalia's festival. There would be thousands of visitors, maybe even tens of thousands. The vestibule creates a quasi-subterranean space where one finds votive statues, tombs, altars and other religious paraphernalia. There's a small fountain that periodically dribbles sacred water gathered from the drippings in the cave. A woman had brought empty water bottles to fill with the revered liquid. Beside this was a huge iron anchor dedicated by Palermitan sailors invoking the saint's aid in keeping their ships safe. This anchor is incongruously festooned with baby pillows, bibs, and all manner of baby-related things in pink and blue, giving thanks for the healthy birth of a child. I'm not sure how that relates to sailors, but…oh…never mind.

Fertility, in fact, seems to be a major theme, as nearby on a stone shelf women have triumphantly bequeathed used pregnancy test kits, presumably the ones that revealed the good news, which I thought completely bizarre and a bit gross. One of them had been there so long it was growing mold in the grotto's humid atmosphere. Beside them crumpled packs of cigarettes are arranged, left in thanks for the saint providing the strength to quit smoking. Someone had bequeathed a trophy of a bronzed soccer shoe; presumably Rosalia had helped score a tournament-winning goal. Baskets were filled to brims with letters written by children beseeching the saint's intercession. A little girl named Elena left a letter, written in red wax crayon, thanking her for healing her broken arm and letting the saint know she finally got her cast off. There was a display case containing myriad body parts in tin, little *ex votos* one could offer for any ailment: breasts if one had breast cancer, hearts for coronary problems, legs, arms, heads, stomachs, and kidneys. I suspect if you went to the gift store and asked for a pancreas they'd have one in stock, filed under Miscellaneous Organs. I wondered how they handled erectile dysfunction. Blue pill I reckon; there are some things virgin saints don't deal with.

A sign identified a carved depression in the mountain wall just outside the cave's mouth as a Phoenician altar, which means that Rosalia's Catholic altar was preceded by almost two millennia by a Punic one.[28] Monte Pellegrino was a military base for the great Carthaginian general Hamilcar—Hannibal's father—in 246 BCE, and it may be that this cavern was discovered by Carthaginian soldiers who made into a shrine. But it's very likely that even they weren't the first ones here, since there are caves on Monte Pellegrino that were religious centers well before the Carthaginians encamped. On the mountain's eastern faces are the Addaura Caves, in which myriad carvings of human figures, dating from 10,000 BCE, were discovered in the 1940s when Allied forces were looking for safe places to store munitions. The outlines depict people in energetic poses, evoking dancing or gymnastics, and are designed with such naturalism and sensitivity to human movement that Matisse or Picasso could have sketched them. There are also drawings of prehistoric fauna, such as cattle, mountain goats, and horses. The more recent history of the Addaura Caves is not very happy. Today they are abandoned and teenagers have been spraying the caves with graffiti. They were closed with steel fencing in 2004 but in the interim people have broken in again. Around the caves, along the cliffs, climbers have left pitons in the rocks for climbing. These caves are important examples of Paleolithic art and archaeology, but because they never became an important tourist site they've never been properly appreciated.

Santa Rosalia is said to have been the daughter of Sinibaldus, a nobleman of King William I's court. When as a young woman she witnessed the decadence of the courtiers she renounced worldly materialism and hiked to the wilderness of Monte Pellegrino to find a peaceful place where she could spend her days in worship and penitence. In some versions of her story, the Monte Pellegrino cave was her second cave, but who's counting? There she lived her life as a hermit and there in her grotto she died, her body gradually entombed in a crust of limestone from the cave's percolations. It's almost as if her corpse became a recumbent stalactite. There she rested for five centuries until Palermo found itself in the deadly grip of plague and much in need of a powerful saint to intercede and plead for God's mercy. Rosalia's bones were discovered and brought into Palermo, where the Black Death eventually receded, confirming Rosalia as the city's savior.

An elderly couple in the grotto was taking their visit very seriously, sitting in the pews with lowered heads and reverent silence, so I waited outside until they finished their devotions. I wondered what had happened to make them so sad and requiring the saint's assistance. They eventually left, heads still hung, their anxiety still palpable, the burden still weighing heavily on their shoulders. When I finally entered the cave I was happy to see the ceiling just as Goethe had described it when he visited on Thursday, April 5th of 1787: "… as the rocks drip incessantly with water, it was necessary to keep the place dry. This has been effected by means of tin tubes, which are fastened to every projection of the rock, and in various ways connected with each other. As they are broad above, and come to a narrow edge below … the water is conducted into a clear reservoir, out of which it is taken by the faithful as a remedy and preventative for every kind of ill." It struck me as remarkable that I could find this place exactly as Goethe described it two hundred and twenty-seven years before. Descendants of those tin troughs still decorate the cave, making it look like a Dadaist interior (the ceiling resembles Kurt Schwitters' *Merzbau* in Hannover from 1933), and they still sluice the sacred water into the stone font for the faithful to partake of, with Euro coins glistening at the bottom like golden offerings. In one part of the cave people had written prayers on pieces of paper and shoved them into the cracks in the rocks, like they do at the Wailing Wall in Jerusalem. I was tempted to pry one out in the name of research but resisted my sacrilegious curiosity.

The focus of devotion in the cave isn't really the altar but the shrine that houses the statue of Santa Rosalia, sculpted by Gregorio Tedeschi in 1625; a marble likeness that purportedly rests exactly where the saint's calcified skeleton was discovered. A pillared canopy shelters a large container with walls of glass, like a terrarium. The effigy of the saint reclines inside, a cupidic angel hovering over her and holding a stalk of lilies, symbols her virginity. She cradles her head in her hand and her mouth is open, as if in spiritual ecstasy, anticipating the swooning expression of Bernini's famous statue of St Teresa by twenty years. The statue is adorned in a resplendent golden robe, donated by King Charles III of Spain in 1748. It made me wonder what she was wearing underneath. Wait, that sounds bad, let me rephrase—I mean, I wonder what sculpted 'clothing' the sculpture had before the golden mantle was draped over it. The enclosure is also filled with religious tchotchkes like a golden skull (a *memento mori* or 'reminder of death'), a monstrance with a fragment of one of the saint's bones, and several silver roses as the rose was, sensibly, Rosalia's symbol. She wears a garland of them in her hair and they also decorate her robe. She has several golden bracelets and a huge gold ring. Given the fact that the saint had renounced the materialism of the world, had the Palermitani not removed her from her grave she'd no doubt be rolling over in it. Even worse, one section is for cash donations and there must have been thousands of Euros in there.

I hate to be ever the skeptic, but the likelihood that the bones found in this cave were really the bones of a medieval female hermit is extremely slim. More likely—and I apologize profusely to the faithful of Palermo—is that they were the fossilized bones of a dwarf elephant or mammoth, animals that were common on pre-Neolithic Sicily. In fact, dwarf elephants and even 'pygmy' hippopotami have been found on many other Mediterranean islands, such as Malta, Crete and Cyprus. When humans first arrived on these islands they found these defenseless creatures easy prey and good sources of meat, hunting them to extinction in a few centuries. The bones were often disposed of in heaps. It's probable that Santa Rosalia's cave was inhabited by Neolithic people and the bones are from an elephant they killed and ate in their cave. It wouldn't be the first time fossil bones of dwarf elephants have been taken as the relics of saints. On Cyprus there is still a cave shrine on the north coast where there's an outcrop of fossil dwarf elephant bones. Local legend claims they are the bones of St Phanarios and his horse. They, too, are associated with a nearby cave shrine.

Four young women came in, whispering happily. Locals, I reckoned. Maybe one had a pregnancy test kit in her purse. I had seen enough so walked back to the road. Business hadn't improved for the souvenir vendors and I had some time to kill so I went to the Café Costantino nearby and had lunch and a cup of coffee. The proprietors were friendly and they let me sit there for a while and write in my travel diary. Finally, the bus came, the driver took a ten-minute break, then we headed back to town, swerving down the slopes of Monte Pellegrino like a winding river before flowing gently back onto the level streets of Palermo.

I was sad to not be here during the festival of Santa Rosalia, but also partly relieved since I'm not a big fan of crowds or blistering heat. The festival takes place in early July, just when Palermo is too hot for comfort. But it's Palermo's most important and biggest festival. The huge silver reliquary is taken from the chapel in the cathedral and rolled through the town. The whole city comes into the streets. It's a sight travelers from many ages have witnessed and been impressed by, such as the French traveler De Saint Non in 1778, who gives a detailed account:

"The procession is opened by a wagon drawn by forty mules, and loaded with as many musicians, who make all the noise they can, mounted on this enormous machine, the loftiest ever placed on wheels, and which is higher than any house in the city. It sets out from the Marino, and crosses the Cassaro, from the Porta Felice to the palace of the viceroy, before which a splendid fire-work is played off, and the ceremony concludes with an illumination of the Cassaro, which is decorated alternately with porticos and fountains. This street (the Cassaro), nearly a mile long on a concave surface, is visible in its whole length, and presents a most magnificent sight. The populace celebrates the festival till midnight, where they are succeeded by the carriages and the nobility."

He also vividly describes one of the additional events, horse races up the Cassaro that begin at the Porta Felice, with boys as young as eight years as jockeys. But when W. H. Smyth visits thirty years later in 1810 he notes that the horses have no riders. Perhaps there was a tragic accident. He, too, was impressed with the procession: "The anniversary of this auspicious event [Rosalia's intercession] has ever since been pompously celebrated by brilliant illuminations, splendid fireworks, and the procession of a lofty car, floridly decorated with various allegorical figures, surmounted at the height of sixty feet by the statue of Santa Rosalia, and drawn slowly up the Cassaro by fifty oxen, with a band of music in front." The images of pageantry and action are much at odds with the contemplative place I just visited on Monte Pellegrino. I was thinking of these revelries, wondering what they had been like in decades and centuries past, wondering if I'd ever get the chance to be in Palermo at that time of year, when the bus arrived at my stop. Daydreaming, I'd almost missed it.

I got off at the Piazza Verdi in front of the Teatro Massimo, just two hundred meters from the Casa Sicilia, and that was that; my time in Palermo was done. When I went into my room I sighed, knowing I'd have to organize my things as I had a shuttle to the airport at the ungodly hour of 3:30 am for the 6:00 am flight to Rome, where I'd catch my connecting flight back to the U. S. When I'm traveling I always think it'll last forever, and I'm always mildly shocked when it's suddenly over. I don't like packing, perhaps because I've had to do it so often. I live a life out of suitcases and I often dream of a place of my own where I can put my socks in drawers. I took some laundry off the line and languidly began folding clothes and pressing them lightly into the bottom of the suitcase.

☙

SOURCES

So as not to encumber the text with many citation numbers I've arranged the sources below with a short reference. Readers can refer to the bibliography for the full citations. The references appear in the order they are used in the chapters. Some elaborative notes have been retained in the text.

Sources for Introduction

Eberstadt, "The Palace and the City", p. 42; Stille, *Excellent Cadavers*; Robb, *Midnight in Sicily*.

Sources for Day One

Lampedusa, *The Leopard*, pp. 19-22; Eberstadt, "The Palace and the City", p. 45; de Maupassant, *Sicily*, p. 9; Musson, *Sicily*, p. 76; Hill, *Observations and Remarks*, p. 40; Smith, *A History of Sicily*, p. 184; Goethe, *Letters from Switzerland Travels in Italy*, p. 274; Salomon, *Van Dyck in Sicily*, p. 28; Henningsen, "The Witch's Flying and the Spanish Inquisitors, pp. 57-74; Smith, *A History of Sicily*, p. 167-8; Payne Knight, *Expedition into Sicily*, p. 36; Goethe, *Letters from Italy*, p. 279, 277, 285-88, 283-4; de Maupassant, *Sicily*, p. 10; Brydone, *A Tour through Sicily and Malta*, p. 239; Hager, *Picture of Palermo*, p. 36; Metcalfe, *Muslims and Christians in Norman Sicily*, p. 19; Smith, *A History of Sicily*, p. 42; [Pseudo] Hugo Falcandus, *The History of the Tyrants of Sicily*, p. 220; Mètcalfe, *Muslims and Christians in Sicily*, pp. 47-8; Jamison, *Admiral Eugenius of Sicily*, pp. 40-43; Pezzini, "Palermo in the 12th Century", p. 215; Ibn Hawqal, *Portrait of the World*; Mandalà, "The Jews of Palermo", p. 463; *Other Routes*, p. 67; Jubayr, *The Travels of Ibn Jubayr*, p. 342, 339-40, 337-8; *Other Routes*, p. 69; Jubayr, *The Travels of Ibn Jubayr*, p. 341; Taylor, *Muslims in Medieval Sicily*; Mandala, "The Jews of Palermo", p. 440; Tudela, *The Itinerary of Rabbi Benjamin Tudela*, p. 160; Lampedusa, *The Leopard*, pp. 318-9; *The Liber Augustalis or Constitutions of Melfi*, pp. 146-8; Loud, *Roger II and the Creation of the Kingdom of Sicily*, pp. 314-328; Fentriss, *Rebels and Mafiosi*, p. 9; Hutton, *Cities of Sicily*, p. 200; de Maupassant, *Sicily*, pp. 60-1; Jamison, *Admiral Eugenius of Sicily*, pp. 33-35, 39-40; Loud, *Roger II and the Creation of the Kingdom of Sicily*, p. 360; Goethe, *Letters from Italy*, p. 277; Loud, *Roger II and the Creation of the Kingdom of Sicily*, pp. 264-5; Hutton, *Cities of Sicily*, p. 206.

Sources for Day 2

Loud, *Roger II and the Creation of the Kingdom of Sicily*, p. 358; Strutt, *A Pedestrian Tour in Calabria and Sicily*, p. 325; Smith, *A History of Sicily*, p. 61; Frederick II Hohenstaufen, *De Arte Venandi cum Avibus* [*The Art of Hunting with Birds*]; de Saint-Non, *Travels in Sicily and Malta*, pp. 117-8; del Bufalo, *Porphyry: Red Imperial Porphyry: Power and Religion*; Loewenthal, "For the Biography of Walter Ophamil," pp. 75-82; Smith, *A History of Sicily*, pp. 47-8; Dickie, *Cosa Nostra*, p. 89;

Hager, *Picture of Palermo,* pp. 14-15; Schwartz, "The Anchor", pp. 76-85.

Sources for Day 3

Tudela, *The Itinerary of Benjamin Tudela,* pp. 160-61; Edge and Gibbins, "Underwater Discovery of Roman Surgical Equipment," pp. 1645-46; Hager, *Picture of Palermo,* p. 60, 61, 59; Ibn Jubayr, *The Travels of Ibn Jubayr,* p. 348; Bagnera, "The Urban Evolution of Islamic Palermo", pp. 79-80; "The Devils of the Zisa" and "The Treasure of the Zisa" in *The Collected Sicilian Folk and Fairy Tales of Giuseppe Pitrè,* pp. 701 & 796; de Maupassant, *Sicily,* p. 13, 15; Hill, *Observations and Remarks,* pp. 26-7; Dryden, *A Voyage to Sicily and Malta,* pp. 96-100; Brydone, *A Tour Through Sicily and Malta,* p. 257; Smyth, *Memoir Descriptive of the Resources,* p. 88; Salomon, *Van Dyck in Sicily,* p. 25; Ibn Hawqal, *Portrait of the World;* Galt, *Voyages and Travels,* p. 57; Sciascia, "Palermo as a Stage", p. 299; Dryden, *Voyage in Sicily and Malta,* pp. 101-2; Borsook, *Messages in Mosaic,* p. 85; Bernard of Clairvaux, *Apologia,* 12:28-29; Sheppard , "The Iconography of the Cloister of Monreale", pp. 159-169; Sheppard, "A Stylistic Analysis of the Cloister at Monreale", pp. 35-41; Salvini, *The Cloister of Monreale;* Strutt, *A Pedestrian's Tour,* p. 329; Bresc, "Palermo in the 14-15th Century, pp. 251-53; Borsook, *Messages in Mosaic,* p. 85; Krönig, *The Cathedral of Monreale,* p. 85; de Maupassant, *Sicily,* p. 21-22; Brodeck, "Monreale from its Origin", p. 392; Strutt, *A Pedestrian's Tour,* p. 332.

Sources for Day 4

Brydone, *A Tour Through Sicily and Malta,* p. 232; Hager, *Picture of Palermo,* pp. 88-9; Brydone, *A Tour Through Sicily and Malta,* pp. 236-7; Hill, *Observations and Remarks,* p. 43; Stoddard, *Lectures, Sicily,* p. 33; Buonanno, *Sicilian Epic and the Marionette Theater,* p. 14-15; Smyth, *Sicily and Its Islands,* p. 78; de Maupassant, *Sicily,* p. 4; Hutton, *Cities of Sicily,* p. 189; Tronzo, *The Cultures of His Kingdom,* p. 30; Loud, *Roger II and the Making of the Kingdom of Sicily,* p. 264; Borsook, *Messages in Mosaic,* p. 21; Jamison, *Admiral Eugenius of Sicily,* p. 119, 121; Ibn Jubayr, *The Travels of Ibn Jubayr,* p. 339; Afulabia, "The Crown and the Economy under Roger II and his Successors," p. 1; Smith, *A History of Sicily,* p. 25, 47.

Sources for Day 5

Maggio, *Mattanza,* p. 35; Maggio, *Mattanza,* pp. 135 & 137; Bresc, "Palermo in the 14-15th Century", pp. 253-55; Maggio, *Mattanza,* pp. 61 & 67; Maggio, *Mattanza,* p. 81; Gilmore, *The Last Leopard,* p. 27; Dickie, *Cosa Nostra,* p. 100.

Sources for Day 6

Eberstadt, "The Palace and the City", p. 67; Hager, *Picture of Palermo,* pp. 37-8; Hager, *Picture of Palermo,* p. 35, 50; Brydone, *A Tour Through Sicily and Malta,* p. 242; Hill, *Observations and Remarks,* p. 34; Dryden, *A Voyage to Sicily and Malta,* pp. 93-4; Loud & Wiedemann, *The History of the Tyrants of Sicily by 'Hugo Falcandus'*, p. 15, 60; Kitzinger, *The Mosaics of St. Mary's of the Admiral in Palermo*, pp. 27-67; Kitzinger, *The Mosaics of St. Mary's of the Admiral in Palermo*, p. 52; Broadhurst, *The Travels of Ibn Jubayr*, p. 349; Kitzinger, *The Mosaics of St. Mary's of the Admiral in Palermo*, p. 317; Smith, *A History of Sicily*, pp. 70-1; Blok, *The Mafia of a Sicilian Village*, pp. 90-98; Hughes, *Travels in Sicily, Greece and Albania*, p. 4; Lampedusa, *The Leopard*, p. 209; Lampedusa, *The Leopard*, pp. 46, 40; Lampedusa, *The Leopard*, pp. 46-47, 79, 80-1; Blok, *The Mafia of a Sicilian Village*, p. 93; Lampedusa, *The Leopard*, p. 40; Schneider & Schneider, *Reversible Destiny*, p. 34, 40-1; Gilmore, *The Last Leopard*, p. 156; Gilmore, *The Last Leopard*, image opp. p. 116; Gilmore, *The Last Leopard*, p. 180.

Sources for Day 7

Schneider & Schneider, *Reversible Destiny*, pp. 169-72; Dickie, *Cosa Nostra*, pp. 268-277; Sandys, *A Relation of a Journey Begun in 1610*, p. 238; Brydone, *A Tour Through Sicily and Malta*, pp. 38-9; Brydone, *A Tour Through Sicily and Malta*, p. 236; Hager, *Picture of Palermo*, p. 85; Smith, *A History of Sicily*, p. 147, 149-50; Francetti and Sonnino, *La Sicilia nel 1876*; Lampedusa, *The Leopard*, pp. 197-8; Schneider and Schneider, *Reversible Destiny*, p. 50; Dickie, *Cosa Nostra*, pp. 35-67; Dickie, *Cosa Nostra*, p. 39; Dickie, *Cosa Nostra*, pp. 39-44; Schneider & Schneider, *Reversible Destiny*, pp. 67-72; Schneider & Schneider, *Reversible Destiny*, pp. 68-9; Schneider & Schneider, *Reversible Destiny*, pp. 148-9; Stille, et. al. *Letizia Battaglia. Passion, Justice, Freedom*; Goldberg, "Testimony of a Keen Witness to

Sicily's Enduring Sorrow"; Dickie, *Cosa Nostra,* pp. 263 & 267; Schneider & Schneider, *Reversible Destiny,* pp. 160-91 & 204-5; Dickie, *Cosa Nostra,* pp. 112-134; Schneider & Schneider, *Reversible Destiny,* pp. 174-4 & 195-6; Dickie, *Cosa Nostra,* pp. 148-159; Strutt, *A Pedestrian's Tour in Calabria and Sicily.*

Sources for Departure

Goethe, *The Complete Works,* pp. 281-82; de Saint Non, *Travels in Sicily and Malta,* pp. 125-7; Smyth, *Memoir Descriptive of the Resources,* p. 85.

ENDNOTES

[1]Each of these quarters has variant names. For example the Seralcadi is also known as 'Monte di Pieta'; the Loggia as 'Castellamare', the Albergheria as 'Palazzo Reale', and the Kalsa as 'Tribunali'.

[2]There's an interesting section of *The Leopard,* taking place many centuries later, of course, in the 1860s, where a cleric has the unpleasant duty of informing the survivors of the recently deceased Prince of Salina that only five of their over seventy 'priceless' holy relics are genuine. Lampedusa, *The Leopard,* pp. 318-9.

[3]James Fentriss notes: "The Teatro Massimo was closed for repairs in 1964. The repairs were supposed to last several months, but for over thirty years successive Palermo administrations managed to buy patronage and political support for themselves by sucking huge sums from the national government for the restoration." From *Rebels and Mafiosi. Death in a Sicilian Landscape* (Ithaca & London: Carnell University Press, 2000), p. 9.

[4]The word is from the Latin *ammiratus ammiratorum,* and Italian *ammiraglio degli ammiragli*: 'Admiral of Admirals', hence the name often used for the church, *Santa Maria dell'Ammiraglio.* The other common designation for the church is the Martorana, a name derived from Eloise Martorana, the founding Abbess of the cloister of Benedictine nuns who used

the church for several centuries. The abbey itself had been known as the 'Martorana' after its founder. The church is also sometimes referred to as 'St Nicholas of the Greeks' or *San Niccolò dei Greci*. St Nicholas is the patron saint of sailors, so churches dedicated to him are often found in port cities. See a description of the office of the Admiral in Evelyn Jamison, *Admiral Eugenius of Sicily* (London: Oxford University Press, 1957), pp. 33-35 and 39-40.

[5]It's still possible to visit the lonely quarry in Egypt, once guarded by a Roman fortress (its ruins also still visible), where a few blocks lie abandoned by the vanished empires that once prized them: a column drum, a rectangular block, but mostly fist-sized chunks and scraps no longer useful; their rich purple bleached out to a pale tan by twenty centuries of unrelenting desert sun.

[6]Medieval Christian churches often used complex inlaid stone designs in their pavements, the most common style is called *cosmati* pavements (or *Cosmatesque* work; named after the 13th century Roman family who invented the designs and who passed down the skills from father to son), a sort of *opus sectile* (inlaid cut stone) work in geometric patterns often arranged around a porphyry disc. A well-known 13th century example is in front of the altar in Westminster Abbey in England.

[7]It's probably not his real name. Many popular texts refer to him as 'Walter of the Mill', which has been derived from or led to the variations 'Offamil' or

'Ophamil'. See L. J. A. Loewenthal, "For the Biography of Walter Ophamil, Bishop of Palermo," *English Historical Review* v. 87, no. 342 (Jan. 1972): pp. 75-82. Loewenthal sees the false surname as a corruption of the word *familiarus*, an honorific used to indicate William's rank. He prefers simply to call him William of Palermo.

[8]Cannoli—from the Latin *canna*, meaning 'tube'—are cylinders of pastry filled with cream. It's claimed that they were invented in Palermo in the Middle Ages.

[9]If you want to see what an old-time Sicilian tuna processing looked like, the closest good one is the *Tonnara di Scopello* on the Gulf of Castellammare, thirty miles from Palermo.

[10]A bit of peculiar natural history: in the renaissance period it was thought that the female marten—a furry mink-like mammal—became pregnant by hearing the mating cries of the male marten, through the ear. This is why, during this time, some wealthy women had jewelry depicting a marten's head, signifying their chastity. In the Walters Art Gallery in Baltimore there's a famous example of a golden marten's head from sixteenth-century Italy that once adorned the clothes of a renaissance noblewoman. To make the Holy Spirit connection more concrete, there's a white dove on its snout.

[11]The Palatine chapel is sometimes spoken of as a merging of two churches: one, a Greek Orthodox

eastern section with an apse and dome, and a western section that echoes the columned basilica of a Western, Catholic church. These elements reflect the Orthodox and Catholic architectural traditions, just as the inscriptions in the Pantocrator's open Bible reflect the chapel's dual Catholic (Latin) and Orthodox (Greek) heritages. Mediating the eastern and western parts of the chapel is another Pantocrator, this one in the dome, but he has a closed book. One interpretation of this is that while Christ holds the open book there is still time to repent, but when the book is closed it's too late; the final judgment has begun and you're on the wrong side of the ledger.

[12]John Julius Norwich has two books, by far the best and most readable accounts on the history of the Normans in Sicily from their rise in the Mediterranean to the end of the realm: *The Other Conquest* and *The Kingdom in the Sun*. These take their place among Norwich's other excellent volumes on the history of the Mediterranean and its empires.

[13]Today, it's part of the collection of the Kunsthistorisches Museum in Vienna. It was part of the loot stolen from the treasuries of the royal palace at Palermo after the conquering of the island by the German Henry VI in 1194. As Denis Mack Smith writes, "...the accumulated assets of generations were taken away, and there was mention of a hundred and fifty mules laden with treasure crossing the Alps." Smith, *A History of Sicily*, p. 47.

[14]Outside in a breezeway are a couple of mosaics.

One of them has a female allegorical figure who symbolizes security—of the bank, I suppose—since she carries a safe. In the background shipbuilders indicate the importance of maritime industries. In another a personification of prosperity oversees human labors. She holds a cornucopia, representing the fruits of agriculture, and a trident, representing the riches of the sea. Accordingly, farmers work below and fishermen above. They were done by the mosaicist Alberto Bevilacqua (not to be confused with the more famous filmmaker of the same name) who was born in Palermo in 1896 but died in Rome in 1979.

[15]Franca Florio inspired a 2007 ballet *Franca Florio: Regina di Palermo,* written by Lorenzo Ferrero. As a patron of turn of the century artists, Franca was literally a Palermitan muse in the late 19th and early 20th century.

[16]As this book was going to press, work began on stabilizing the building for the restoration of the mosaic and the Panificio Salvatore Morello.

[17]The city hall is known as the Palazzo Senatorio, Palermo's main civic building; nicknamed the 'Palazzo delle Aquile' because of a big relief of an eagle over the main entrance and other eagles on coats of arms throughout.

[18]Don Garcia was a ship commander under the famous Genoese admiral Adria Doria and later became a hero in the relief of the Ottoman siege of Malta in 1565.

[19]Many peasant revolts had punctuated Sicilian history; the reforms would fail, the early 19th century Bourbons would see many new insurrections. See Anton Blok, *The Mafia of a Sicilian Village*, 1860-1960. *A Study of Violent Peasant Entrepreneurs* (Prospect Heights, Ill.: Waveland Press, 1974), pp. 90-98.

[20]As David Gilmore points out in his biography of Lampedusa, *gattopardo* does not mean 'leopard' in Italian (it's '*leopardo*'), but instead refers to ocelots, servals, or other members of the cat family. However, in local Sicilian dialects the leopard was referred to as *gattopardu*. Gilmore, *The Last Leopard*, p. 156.

[21]Amazingly, but not atypical for criminal investigations in Sicily at the time, Impastato's death, it was suggested, was a suicide. Umberto and Anna made sure that pressure was kept on the authorities to properly investigate Impastato's murder.

[22]See Dickie, *Cosa Nostra*. On the origins of the mafia see the chapter 'The Genesis of the Mafia 1860-1876', pp. 35-67. The book is one of the most accessible and well-researched accounts of the history and culture of the mafia.

[23]Dickie tells the heart wrenching story of Gaspare Galati, one of the first victims of an organized mafia campaign to control the lemon grove he had inherited. Dickie, *Cosa Nostra*, pp. 39-44.

[24]A *lupara* is a sawed-off or short barrel shotgun; its

name means 'for the wolf' ('*lupo*'), as it was a favored instrument for wolf killing in ages past.

[25]The *Anni di Piombo* refer, however, not just to mafia violence in Sicily, but to the violence that struck the whole of Italy as competing extreme ideologies from the right and left vied for political influence. The violence of the mafia wars was overlain over this supplementary ideological violence.

[26]Their wives were also killed in the murders. Pio de la Torre was a Communist Party official who pushed through laws that made it easier to prosecute the mafia and seize their properties. He also supported land reform and the struggle of peasant workers in Sicily. He had also been part of an anti-mafia commission. General Carlo Alberto Dalla Chiesa was a *Caribinieri* general who was sent to Palermo as prefect to fight the mafia. On Dalla Chiesa see Schneider & Schneider, *Reversible Destiny*, pp. 174-4 & 195-6.

[27]The town that would later be the site of another crackdown, this one on the mafiosi of the town, a battle waged by Benito Mussolini's anti-mafia lawman, Cesare Mori, the 'Iron Prefect' of Palermo. See Dickie, *Cosa Nostra*, pp. 148-159.

[28]The word 'Punic' to refer to something made by the Phoenicians derives from the word the Greeks used to call Phoenicians, *Phoinix*, which in later centuries developed into the Latin *Punicus*.

BIBLIOGRAPHY

Afulabia, David. "The Crown and the Economy under Roger II and his Successors," *Dumbarton Oaks Papers* 37 (1983):

Bagnera, Alessandra. "The Urban Evolution of Islamic Palermo. In *A Companion to Medieval Palermo,* edited by Annliese Nef, 61-88. Leiden & Boston: Brill, 2013.

Blok, Anton. *The Mafia of a Sicilian Village,* 1860-1960. *A Study of Violent Peasant Entrepreneurs*. Prospect Heights, Ill.: Waveland Press, 1974.

Borsook, Eve. *Messages in Mosaic: the Royal Programmes of Norman Sicily* 1130-1187. Suffolk: The Boydel Press, 1990.

Bresc, Henri. "Palermo in the 14-15th Century. Urban Economy and Trade." In *A Companion to Medieval Palermo,* edited by Annliese Nef, 235-68. Leiden & Boston: Brill, 2013.

Brydone, Patrick. *A Tour through Sicily and Malta.* London: J. Johnson, 1792.

Bufalo, Dario del, *Porphyry: Red Imperial Porphyry: Power and Religion*. Translated by David Graham and Lara Cox. Turin: Umberto Allemandi, 2013.

Buonanno, Michael. *Sicilian Epic and the Marionette Theater*. Jefferson, N. C.: McFarland & Co, 2014.

Dickie, John. Cosa Nostra. *A History of the Sicilian Mafia*. New York: Palgrave MacMillan, 2005.

Eberstadt, Fernanda. "The Palace and the City", *The New Yorker* (December 23, 1991): 41-84.

Edge, Christopher and David Gibbins. "Underwater Discovery of Roman Surgical Equipment," *British Medical Journal* v. 297, no. 6664 (Dec. 24-31, 1988): 1645-46.

Falcandus, [Pseudo] Hugo. *The History of the Tyrants of Sicily by 'Hugo Falcandus'* 1154-69. Trans. Graham A. Loud & Thomas Wiedemann. Manchester and New York: Manchester University Press, 1998.

Fentriss, James. *Rebels and Mafiosi. Death in a Sicilian Landscape*. Ithaca & London: Carnell University Press, 2000.

Francetti, Leopoldo and Sonnino, Sidney. *La Sicilia nel 1876*. Progetto Manusio, electronic edition, 2006; adapted from the Vallecchi Editore, Firenze edition of 1925.

Frederick II of Hohenstaufen. *De Arte Venandi cum Avibus [The Art of Hunting with Birds]*. Translated by Casey A. Wood and F. Marjorie Fyfe. Stanford University Press, 1943.

Galt, John. *Voyages and travels in the Years 1809, 1810, and 1811*. London: T. Cadell and W. Davies, 1812.

Gilmore, David. *The Last Leopard. A Life of Giuseppe Tomasi di Lampedusa*. London: Eland, 2007.

Goethe, J. W. *The Complete Works of Johann Wolfgang von Goethe in Ten Volumes*, translated by A. J. W. Morrison, Vol. IV, *Letters from Switzerland, Travels in Italy*. New York: Collier & Sons.

Goldberg, Vicki. "Testimony of a Keen Witness to Sicily's Enduring Sorrow," *New York Times* (Dec. 16, 2001).

Hager, Joseph. *Picture of Palermo*. Translated by Mrs. Mary Robinson. London: R. Phillips, 1800.

Henningsen, Gustav. "The Witch's Flying and the Spanish Inquisitors, or, How to Explain (Away) the Impossible", *Folklore* vol. 120, n. 1 (2009): 57-74.

Hill, Rev. Brian. *Observations and Remarks in a Journey through Sicily and Calabria in the Year 1791*. London: John Stockdale, 1792.

Hughes, Rev. Thomas Smart. *Travels in Sicily, Greece and Albania*, 2 vols. London: J. Mawman, 1820.

Jamison, Evelyn. *Admiral Eugenius of Sicily*. London: Oxford University Press, 1957.

Ibn Hawqal. *Portrait of the World*. Translated Alex Metcalfe, 2005 , found at www.medievalsicly.com. Accessed Nov. 19, 2014.

Ibn Jubayr, *The Travels of Ibn Jubayr*. Ed. & trans. R. J. C. Broadhurst. London: Jonathan Cape, 1952.

Kitzinger, Ernst. *The Mosaics of St. Mary's of the Admiral in Palermo*. Washington D. C.: Dumbarton Oaks Studies 27, 1990.

Knight, Richard Payne. *Expedition into Sicily*. Ed. Claudia Stumpf. London: British Museum Publications, 1986.

Krönig, Wolfgang. *The Cathedral of Monreale and Norman Architecture in Sicily*. Palermo: S. F. Flaccovio, 1965.

Lampedusa, Giuseppe Tomasi di. *The Leopard*. Trans. Archibald Colquhoun. New York: Pantheon Books, 1988.

Loewenthal, L. J. A. "For the Biography of Walter Ophamil, Bishop of Palermo," *English Historical Review* v. 87, no. 342 (Jan. 1972): 75-82.

Loud, G. A., Al Idrisi, *The Book of Roger*, from *Roger II and the Creation of the Kingdom of Sicily*. Manchester: Manchester University Press, 2012 [check]

Maggio, Theresa. *Mattanza: Love and Death in the Sea*

of Sicily. Cambridge, Mass.: Perseus, 2000.

Malgouyres, Philippe and Clément Blanc-Riehl. *Porphyre: La Pierre Pourpre des Ptolémées à Bonaparte*. Paris: Reunion des musées nationaux, 2003.

Mandalà, Giuseppe. "The Jews of Palermo from Late Antiquity to the Expulsion 598-1492-3." In *A Companion to Medieval Palermo*, edited by Annliese Nef, 437-88. Leiden & Boston: Brill, 2013.

Metcalfe, Alex. *Muslims and Christians in Norman Sicily*. London & New York: Routledge, 2003.

Maupassant, Guy de. *Sicily*. Translated and edited by Robert W. Berger. New York: Italica Press, 2007.

Musson, Spencer. *Sicily*. London: A. & C. Black, 1911.

Pezzini, Elena. "Palermo in the 12th Century: Transformations in Forma Urbis." In *A Companion to Medieval Palermo*, ed. Annliese Nef, 195-232. Leiden & Boston: Brill, 2013.

Robb, Peter. *Midnight in Sicily. On Art, Food, History, Travel, and La Cosa Nostra*. Boston & London: Faber and Faber, 1996.

Saint Non, Jean Claude Richard de. *Travels in Sicily and Malta*. London: G. G. J. and J. Robinson, 1789 [English translation of *Voyage pittoresque ou Description des Royaumes de Naples et de Sicile*, Paris: 1788].

Salomon, Xavier F. *Van Dyck in Sicily: 1624-1625, Painting and the Plague*. Milano: Silvana Editoriale, 2012.

Salvini, Roberto. *The Cloister of Monreale and Romanesque Sculpture in Sicily*. Palermo: S. F. Flaccovio, 1962.

Sandys, George. *A Relation of a Journey Begun in 1610 in Four Books…* London: W. Barrett, 1620.

Schneider, Jane C. and Peter T. *Reversible Destiny. Mafia, Antimafia, and the Struggle for Palermo*. Berkeley: University of California Press, 2003.

Schwartz, Mattathias. "The Anchor" *The New Yorker* (April, 21, 2014): 76-85.

Sheppard Jr, Carl D. "The Iconography of the Cloister of Monreale," *The Art Bulletin* v. 31, no. 3 (Sept. 1949): 159-169.

Sheppard Jr, Carl D. "A Stylistic Analysis of the Cloister at Monreale," *The Art Bulletin* v. 34, no. 1 (March, 1952): 35-41.

Smith, Denis Mack. *A History of Sicily. Medieval Sicily 800-1713*. New York: Viking Press, 1968.

Smyth, Capt. William Henry. *Memoir Descriptive of the Resources, Inhabitants, and Hydrography of Sicily and its Islands Interspersed with Antiquarian and Other*

Notices. London: John Murray, 1824.

Stille, Alexander. *Excellent Cadavers. The Mafia and the Death of the First Italian Republic*. New York: Pantheon, 1995.

Stille, Alexander. et. al., *Letizia Battaglia. Passion, Justice, Freedom. Photographs of Sicily*. New York: Aperture Books, 1999.

Stoddard, John L. *John L. Stoddard's Lectures, Sicily*. Boston: Balch Brothers, 1909.

Strutt, Arthur John, *A Pedestrian's Tour in Calabria and Sicily*, London: T. C. Newby, 1842.

Taylor, Julie. *Muslims in Medieval Sicily: the Colony at Lucera*. Lanham, Md., 2003.

Tronzo, William. *The Cultures of His Kingdom. Roger II and the Cappella Palatina in Palermo*. Princeton: Princeton University Press, 1997.

Tudela, Rabbi Benjamin. *The Itinerary of Rabbi Benjamin Tudela*. Translated and edited by Marcus Nathan Adler. New York: Hakesheth, 1907.

Roger II and the Making of the Kingdom of Sicily. Edited and translated Graham A. Loud. Manchester: Manchester University Press, 2012.

The Collected Sicilian Folk and Fairy Tales of Giuseppe Pitrè. Translated & edited by Jack Zipes and Joseph Russo. New York and London: Routledge, 2009.

The Liber Augustalis or Constitutions of Melfi Promulgated by the Emperor Frederick II for the Kingdom of Sicily in 1231. Translated by James M. Powell. New York: Syracuse University Press, 1971.

Other Routes: 1500 Years of African and Asian Travel Writing, eds. T. Khair, M. Leer, J. D. Edwards, H. Ziadeh. Oxford: Signal Books, 2006.

Made in the USA
San Bernardino, CA
10 May 2019